Creating Curriculum

Creating Curriculum

Teachers and Students as a Community of Learners

Kathy G. Short
University of Arizona

Carolyn Burke
Indiana University

With a Foreword by Jerome C. Harste

HEINEMANN Portsmouth, NH

Heinemann
A division of Reed Elsevier Inc.
361 Hanover Street, Portsmouth, NH 03801-3912
Offices and agents throughout the world

Library of Congress Cataloging-in-Publication Data

Short, Kathy Gnagey.
    Creating curriculum : teachers and students as a community of
learners / by Kathy G. Short and Carolyn Burke.
        p.   cm.
    Includes bibliographical references.
    ISBN 0-435-08590-5
    1. Education—United States—Curricula. 2. Education—Social
aspects—United States. 3. Curriculum change—United States.
I. Burke, Carolyn L. II. Title.
LB1570.S534 1991
375'.00973—dc20   91-15145
                                 CIP

Designed by Jenny Jensen Greenleaf
Printed in the United States of America
99 98 97 96 95   10 9 8 7 6 5 4

Contents

Acknowledgments

As we wrote this book, we were constantly aware of the powerful impact of many other individuals and groups on our thinking. Fleck (1935) argues that any event, such as this book, can only be understood by examining its socio-historical roots, in particular thought collectives. These thought collectives are communities of people who learn to think together through mutually exchanging ideas and maintaining intellectual dialogue. Our memberships in various thought collectives have impacted both the current insights and limitations of our thinking. The authorship of this book is not ours alone but is shared by members of those significant communities which have supported and challenged our thinking.

All of us have natural thought collectives such as colleagues, family, and friends that we draw on. We want to thank the special people in our lives who have provided both personal and professional support. These groups form the platform on which we build to purposefully develop our own thought collectives and collaborators.

We especially want to acknowledge the thought collectives we have purposefully constructed for ourselves. We did not wait to be invited into these communities, we actively sought membership in them and created our own collectives when the ones we needed did not exist. We realize the value of our memberships in collectives such as CELT (Center for the Expansion of Thinking and Language), TAWL (Teachers Applying Whole Language), TAWL Umbrella, and the graduate students at our respective institutions. We have drawn heavily on our interactions and dialogue with members of these collectives and are very aware of what we owe them. In addition, professional organizations such as NCTE, IRA, and NRC have provided us with powerful forums and meeting places for exchanging ideas with others.

We want to give special thanks to Gloria Kauffman and her students who contributed so many of their thoughts to this text. Other classroom teachers who shared comments from their students are Kaylene Yoder, Jan Holsopple, and Junardi Armstrong. The powerful voices of their students continuously remind all of us as teachers that our most important collaborators continue to be our students and co-learners.

Since none of our thought collectives have ever been the "silent" type, we are sure we will hear from you as you read and respond to our thoughts in this book. We look forward to continuing the dialogue with you that has meant so much to our intellectual lives.

Kathy Short
Carolyn Burke

Foreword

Jerome C. Harste
Indiana University

The function of a foreword, like the function of curriculum, is to give perspective. What Carolyn Burke and Kathy Short do for curriculum, therefore, I hope to do for their book.

When I think about curriculum, there are four major sources that inform how I think through and develop curriculum. The first is the *disciplines* or what is currently known about a subject. If the topic I'm interested in is "immigration," I ask myself questions such as, "What would an anthropologist want to know about this topic? What would a biologist contribute? What would a psychologist want to know?" and so on.

The second source is *alternate sign systems* (language, art, music, mathematics, dance) and what each of these can potentially contribute to our understanding of the topic. I try, in this regard, to envision what "immigration" might look like if done in music, in art, in math, in pantomime, in drama, and so on. At this point, I also try to identify particularly powerful poems and pieces of literature having to do with the topic. These I will either read or make available in text sets for students to read and discuss in class.

The third source is *learning theory* or what it is I know about the process people go through when learning something new. Because I am a language educator, I am particularly interested in the role that language plays in supporting the key functions of learning such as making personal connections, naming the world, reflecting on one's own or another's constructs, etc.

The fourth source of curriculum for me is *the nature of schooling in our society*. I always try to remember that this is a democracy and that I am here to help all students gain a voice, not silence them as schools have been so good at doing in the past. One of the key questions I ask is, "What kinds of connections do I predict my students will be able to make with this topic?" I try to begin from there as I know that no one has ever become literate in an area without first becoming personally involved.

Now, I will be the first to admit that my ideas for curriculum come from many people. But, what I find surprising, in light of this volume, is that two of my key resources have been Carolyn Burke and Kathy Short! What surprised me was that here, rather than take each of the sources I have just named and explicate them, they shift stances and say the key source is "social learning theory." They then proceed to use it as a synthesizing lens for viewing curriculum in a new light.

I was initially shocked. But they make a powerful argument. They don't ignore my other sources—the disciplines, alternate sign systems, the nature of schooling in our society —but they argue that these are first and foremost social constructs. For example, ideas can flourish only if they resonate with others. New ideas are collaborative. Social structures guide personal beliefs; what has been social becomes internal. New codes are built on old codes forming a social legacy of ideas, forms, and ways of thinking. Language and the symbol systems we use are socially created. Literacy is and always has been influenced and shaped by social collectives.

To understand this book, you have to understand that Burke and Short see the function of a literacy curriculum as supporting key processes in literacy, not the teaching of specific books or particular pieces of content. Given this envisionment, the key source of curriculum is what we know about learning as a social process. And their argument makes sense, for, if you, like Burke and Short, take social learning theory seriously, then all real knowledge and knowing is created collaboratively through interaction between and among learners.

Burke and Short state what they believe and on the basis of these beliefs envision what curriculum might be. Their curriculum helps them not only clarify their beliefs but express what they value. Curriculum ought to do the same for us as well as our students. We too have to take charge of our own curriculum. We too need an envisioned curriculum, and on the basis of our enactments, we can self-correct and grow.

Learning, or the process of change more generally, is social. That's what makes teacher support groups like TAWL (Teachers Applying Whole Language) so powerful. When learners (teachers) support each other, powerful things happen.

To envision a social curriculum, one has to see the teacher as learner and recognize that all the resources we need to change are already at hand. The process begins with curiosity, involves risk, and ends in connected knowing.

My fear is that teachers are going to read this book and say, "Yes, but in my district we have to teach the basal." "Yes, but in Indiana (or New Jersey or wherever) we are held accountable to know children's progress on the state achievement test. Our funding is contingent to their progress." "Yes, but you don't understand. I have no responsibility for the curriculum in my classroom because my principal (or superintendent) refuses to allow me to make those kind of decisions." "Yes, but I work in a conservative community. The parents here like things the way they are."

To help Burke and Short sidetrack the "Yes buts" I want to re-emphasize what I see as the major messages in this volume. First, Burke and Short argue that those intimately involved have to take responsibility for change. Second, they argue that change in classrooms comes from within, not without. As concerned teachers, we can't wait for the environment to change. Nor, thirdly, they argue, is it a sensible thing to close our classroom door and make our own change. A social model of learning calls for making ourselves and our decisions available to others. Fourth, Burke and Short argue that only when learners support each other from the inside can powerful curricular changes be made.

Burke and Short are introducing a new reality. It is a much more powerful one than a "Yes-But Curriculum" can offer. And they even tell us socially how we as learners might collaboratively proceed. I like it because I see that their argument invites children and teachers to collaborate in the development of their own inquiry-based curricula. I join the authors in hoping you do too.

Introduction

At first I thought that this was just a normal room. But it's a room where we care about each other, share information and thoughts. I always wanted to learn from people who were really smart but I can learn from those who don't know more than me. They learn from you while you learn from them. That way you are creating.

Jennifer, Grade 3

Work at school was hard until I discovered I could change the information and make it have meaning for me. When we do real work, I feel that this is real school.

Alicia, Grade 3

Along with Alicia and Jennifer, we have been exploring what it means to have "real school" in a setting where people are engaged in meaningful learning with others. As Jennifer points out, learners need to be in environments where they can work together at creating. We believe that what they are working to create is *curriculum*.

Curriculum is one of those significant sounding words that many educators use when they talk about schools and instruction. The problem with terms like curriculum is that there are as many different definitions as there are educators talking. Because the definition of curriculum varies according to who is speaking, it often gets used to talk *past* other educators rather than *with* them.

As beginning teachers, we assumed that "curriculum" referred to the content prescribed by textbooks, teachers' guides, and school curriculum guides. These guides provided us with lists of skills and facts in particular sequences and with sets of materials to teach those skills and facts. While we brought other ideas and materials into our classrooms, these guides were the "real" curriculum and we were held accountable for their use and for determining which sets of students were ready for particular sets of skills or facts. Everything else was enrichment or supplementary.

When our beliefs about teaching and learning changed and we began exploring process-centered and collaborative approaches in the classroom, our definition of curriculum had to change too. We realized that curriculum was more than the scope and sequence guides but we were not sure what to use in place of those guides. So, by default, curriculum became a set of activities that we used. The problem with this view of curriculum was that we found ourselves choosing a new set of activities each day without a sense of a broader framework that would tie these activities together and support decision making in the classroom. We observed other teachers around us having the same struggles. We were all in an unending cycle of coming up with new theme units, new projects, new reading and writing activities, and new "experts" who could provide us with yet more activities and procedures. Curriculum had become a grab bag of activities from which we pulled randomly every day without a framework to tie those activities together over time or to support negotiation of curriculum with our students.

The educators we found the most helpful in thinking about learning and teaching kept referring to "curriculum" and seemed to use the term effortlessly in their conversations about schools and instruction. We were on the outside, trying to figure out what they meant without appearing ignorant. We began searching for a better understanding of curriculum and for curriculum frameworks that would support our beliefs about learning and teaching. Was curriculum the plans written on paper or what happened in the classroom? Was it what teachers thought about as they planned daily experiences in the classroom? Was it what went on in the minds of learners as they participated in those experiences? Was it the collaboration of all learners, teachers and students, in the classroom setting? How did administrators and outside "experts" relate to the curriculum? What about the school curriculum guides? The questions seemed endless.

Take a few minutes, before we continue this discussion, to reflect on how you currently define curriculum and go about making curricular decisions in your classroom.

In first and second grade, we did skill packs and if we did not know the answer we would tell the teacher and she would say "Read this paragraph and you will find the answer." And now we have literature circles and people push you if you don't talk. And that way we learn more.

Nicole, Grade 3

....

My definition of curriculum:

How do I make my curricular decisions?

....

We began to explore a new understanding of curriculum by examining models of how curriculum is developed and implemented. In traditional models, curriculum has come from the scope and sequence charts, textbooks, teachers' guides, and school and state curriculum guides. Curriculum has been something which experts outside the classroom develop, classroom teachers implement, and students receive. A hierarchy was established that often excluded both teachers and students from actively thinking about learning and curriculum and that often involved attempts to pass down someone else's thinking. Teachers frequently violated their own intuitions to stay within the confines of this predetermined curriculum. Students appeared unmotivated because what was happening in the classroom was so disconnected from their own experiences and interests. They spent their time

Exploring social relationships within curriculum

Outside "Experts"
↓
Teachers
↓
Students

In some other years I've felt like I've been put into a bowl. It was like you had to do what they told you. They tried to form you into a person.

David, Grade 6

Students

Teachers/Other Educators

In this room, we're treated like adults. Our teacher gives us responsibility and then we have to deal with it. We have freedom and choices.

Lark, Grade 6

trying to figure out what the teacher wanted so they could play the game. They thought critically but their thinking was focused on "reading the teacher" rather than on the content and process of learning.

This view of curriculum was frustrating for us as teachers. We often felt that we were spending our time "covering" specific topics and skills rather than in meaningful learning. Once we figured out how to use the teachers' guides, there were few decisions left for us to make. Both we and our students were passive members of the classroom.

We wanted change. Because hierarchy is so much a part of school systems, our first tendency was to reverse the hierarchy and put the student at the top. Let the curriculum "emerge" from student interests while we, as teachers, sat back and served as a resource for their needs. While this view of curriculum put trust in the child as learner, it also eliminated the experience and knowledge that we and other curriculum developers brought to teaching and learning. A new hierarchy did not seem like a positive solution to our dilemma of becoming an active learning community.

As we read Dewey (1938) and continued thinking and learning with our students, we realized that there were other options. Dewey pointed out that many people thought the only alternative to a traditional hierarchy was a liberal viewpoint where students were in charge. He felt that progressive education failed because educators wrongly assumed that it was a liberal curriculum rather than a collaboration of teachers, students, and other educators. We realized that many people today were making this same assumption about whole language and other process-centered approaches. Our focus turned to thinking about how our models of curriculum could move away from hierarchies to collaboration. We needed an understanding of curriculum that was based in fundamentally different social relationships within the classroom.

We began to explore with others how curriculum could be a shared process of teachers and students working together through negotiation. This perspective allows both the teacher's and the students' voices to be heard and built upon in establishing the classroom learning environment. The ideas and knowledge coming from curriculum developers, administrators, and other experts outside the classroom are not ignored but do not solely determine what occurs in the classroom. Instead, insights from these experts outside the classroom are part of the knowledge that the experts inside the classroom use as they think and work together. As teachers, we contribute our experiences and understandings about learning and about our particular students. The students bring their own interests, experiences, and understandings to the process and together we work to negotiate the curriculum which takes place in that classroom.

As classroom teachers, we have the major responsibility for establishing a learning environment that is conducive to the growth of the particular students in our classrooms. We are professionals who make decisions based on a knowledge of teaching and learning and of our specific students. Students become our curricular informants and we need to develop careful "kidwatching" strategies (Goodman, 1978) so that curriculum is built from their experiences and needs. Students are involved as decision makers themselves through having real choices in the kinds of learning experiences in which they engage. They are also involved as reflective learners who think about and discuss their own learning processes and the classroom learning environment with us. The curriculum is not centered on either teachers or students but on learning.

As we examined new collaborative models for developing and implementing curriculum, we also found ourselves understanding more about curriculum but each understanding also brought new questions and issues. Gradually, we came to see that a sense of curriculum was at the heart of our lives as educators, researchers, and learners. While we realized that our understandings of curriculum were fundamental to all of our inquiry, if someone asked us to define curriculum, we experienced sudden wordlessness. Trying to explain a complex concept which is at the heart of everything we do as

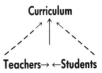

Curriculum

Teachers→ ←Students

Before the teacher's job was to make sure we were on time and did everything right. Teachers were right and students were wrong. But in here, we are in charge of ourselves. We choose what to read, write, and think. We aren't assigned seats or groups. We are allowed to talk about our work. Last year, the things I learned seemed to go in one ear and out the other one. But this year, it stays in my head.

Mark, Grade 3

This year it is sort of nice because when we are talking to the teacher, the teacher listens. We feel good about it and we want to talk more.

Bobbi, Grade 2

There is not just one teacher and all the rest are the learners. Instead, we all are teachers and we all are learners.

Steven, Grade 3

educators is not possible in a few catch phrases. This book is our attempt to put some of our thinking and understandings about curriculum into words so that we can continue our conversations with ourselves and others about the many questions and issues surrounding curriculum.

Putting our beliefs into action

For us, a curriculum involves putting into action a system of beliefs. It is the orchestration of a set of beliefs about learning, knowing, and social relationships. No curriculum (actually, no life experience) is free of the impact of our beliefs. Our day-to-day decisions, whether unconscious or intuitive or conscious, involve the carrying out of our beliefs in action.

If we choose to act either intuitively or unconsciously, we make decisions that are unexamined and untested. There are several risks in such decisions. First, we remain much more tied to what already exists. We tend to support the status quo for the simple reason that it offers immediately available options. These options are part of the "everybody knows" store of knowledge that all of us have available from our experiences as students and teachers. The price of these options is that we must also accept without question the built-in limitations and inadequacies which accompany them. We accept the inadequacies as necessary and unavoidable because it is less threatening and less troublesome to accept known limitations than to risk the unknown advantages of new alternatives. We retain control by maintaining what has already been socially accepted as appropriate classroom teaching techniques.

Second, when we do risk change while operating unconsciously or intuitively, we often base our decisions on the surface attractions of a new set of ideas. We make little or no attempt to understand the internal processes that are at work within those new ideas. This can lead to several confusions. The adjustments can turn out to be merely cosmetic in nature and so all the old limitations remain in operation. A new set of books or a new practice is added without really changing what is happening in the classroom. One of the dangers of this type of "additive" curriculum is that we can inadvertently incorporate a practice into the classroom that is in theoretic conflict with the thrust of the program and that provides mixed messages to our students and to ourselves. In addition, we often are not prepared for the set of problems and adjustments that accompany the new practice. We treat these problems as evidence of failure instead of as evidence of learning and so we abandon what might be a promising engagement. We can begin to flit from enticing practice to enticing practice, from fad to fad.

In contrast, conscious decisions can enable us to make planned changes and adjustments to both our beliefs and our practices. We can reflect on what we are in the process of doing, how that process impacts both ourselves and our students as learners, and on the usefulness and vitality of the artifacts and responses that the process produces. These reflections give both us and our students the ability to control our current engagements and predict new possibilities for future experiences.

I've learned responsibility by scheduling my own time and then I'm responsible for switching subjects. I just don't sit there while the teacher gives sermons.

Traci, Grade 6

The first step in the creation of curriculum, then, is a reflective consideration and re-consideration of what we currently believe so that we can consciously begin to act on those beliefs in consistent and productive ways. This reflection allows curriculum to become a generative system of thinking and feeling. When curriculum consists of acting out someone else's beliefs and practices, that curriculum eventually becomes stagnant. Under these conditions, neither we nor our students have the understandings that will allow us to reflectively think about what we know and what is happening to our learning in order to keep that curriculum alive and growing. The knowledge of outside experts needs to become part of what we reflectively consider in forming our own beliefs, not what we automatically implement in our classrooms. As teachers, we are also experts along with our students on learning, teaching, and research in our own communities of learners.

Reflecting on what we believe

Think about what you do and why you do it.

Floyd, Grade 3

The first section of this book consists of our reflections

on our own belief systems. These beliefs are the basis for the second section which describes the authoring cycle as a practical model of how we have currently been enacting those beliefs in college, secondary, and elementary classrooms. The authoring cycle supports both theory and practice by providing a theoretical framework from which we can generate classroom experiences. The third section will build from the authoring cycle as one model of a curriculum framework to a broader focus on curriculum as a process of inquiry supported by the reflective perspective of evaluation.

Learning as a Social Process

There are three beliefs about people and the ways in which they think that are particularly important to us as curriculum developers. The first, as stated by Frank Smith (1981), is that "Learning is not an occasional event, to be stimulated, provoked or reinforced. Learning is what the brain does naturally, continually" (p. 108). The second Dewey (1938) provided when he said, "Every experience is a moving force. Its value can be judged only on the ground of what it moves toward and into" (p. 38). The third also comes from Dewey who stated that "all human experience is ultimately social: it involves contact and communication" (p. 38).

Learning is a natural and continuing social activity.

These three beliefs provide the basis for how we view the function of schooling and focus how we evaluate the role which schooling plays in education. From our perspective what is unique about school as a cultural institution is not that it is a place where learners gather together. Instead, the uniqueness of school is that it is a place where a community of learners can be given opportunities to be reflective about what and how they are learning.

School is a place where the learning which occurs in the present can act to give new life and vitality to the past and to create new possibilities and plans for the future. The organizational means for this empowerment of the learner is the curriculum.

Curriculum as empowerment

In order to construct a curriculum that empowers learning, we believe we must be able to frame answers to three questions:

9

1. What do we understand about the natural learners who enter our schools?
2. What conditions support and enhance learners?
3. How do learners gain and maintain perspective on their learning?

In this section, we will use these three questions as a framework for reflecting on our current beliefs. The pronoun "we" will be used throughout this chapter to refer to all of us as learners, whether adults or children, engaged in a variety of learning experiences both within and outside of school.

Before reading this section, take a few minutes and jot down some of your current beliefs about learning, knowing, and social relationships. How would you answer the three questions posed above? As you read on in this section, use your responses to form your perspective in reacting to and reflecting on our beliefs as we share them.

....

MY BELIEFS. . .

. . . about natural learners:

. . . about the conditions that support learners:

. . . about how learners gain perspective on their learning:

....

The Natural Learner

Learning isn't something that the individual comes to be able to do. Learning is synonymous with life. Some theorists go so far as to characterize it as "uncontrollable." The brain naturally functions to turn events into meaning. It does this unobtrusively, intuitively, and non-stop. We never need to question, "Will our students learn?" They are learning all the time, although maybe not what we think they should learn. The question we need to be concerned about asking ourselves is: "*What* are they learning?"

To be able to construct curriculum which supports and enhances the "non-stop" nature of the learning process, we need to look at three characteristics of natural learners: curiosity, intentionality, and sociability.

Curiosity
Intentionality
Sociability

Curiosity We attend to life, constantly looking outward into the world to see what is happening. As we observe what is going on around us, we build mental connections between ourselves and the world. These connections are what allow us to create the understandings about the world that we use to guide our lives. As we search for these connections, our attention is especially drawn to the ambiguous—to the structures or relationships that appear to be incomplete or flawed. It is the "yet to be understood" that fascinates us and serves the demands of our brains.

As curious beings, we are eager and persistent, searching in many directions at one time. Seeking, reaching out is a joy, not a chore. This joy of curiosity is especially evident in young children who spend hours exploring why a particular shape won't fit into certain kinds of holes or how to get a toy to move in a specific way. This same behavior is evident in children and adults as they play with a new video game, trying every possibility to discover their way through the mazes.

I learn by watching others, working with them. I'm a pest. I ask questions to figure things out.

Megan, Grade 3

Fascination with what we do not yet understand

We will pursue the puzzle of ambiguities as long as we have a need and until we find a working solution. Once we have created a whole structure that displays an internal logic and that is useful in explaining a puzzling situation for the moment, we are satisfied and our attention turns elsewhere. After finishing a mystery, we may go back and reconsider some of the clues until we feel that we understand the book. We feel the need to create a unified story where everything fits together in some way. The video game loses its appeal

11

ng at
   l and
   .. is needed,
..ny it's needed, and how it's
used.

Jason, Grade 3

once we know how to consistently get through the maze; our attention then turns to new games with more complex problems to solve.

Once we have created a working solution, only outside coercion or an unexpected and/or non-functional response will draw our attention back to the situation. When others who have more social power are not satisfied with our working solution, they may use that power to force us to reconsider a solution which we see as useful for that moment. Or our working solution may fall apart because of new information, as often happens in mystery stories where new clues or the discovery of a new body eliminates the prime suspect.

Our attention to ambiguities and to exploring solutions to those ambiguities leads us as learners to *expect* our own growth, rather than to be surprised by it. To be a natural learner is to be in a state of constant growth as one question leads to another.

Intentionality Our curiosity leads us to construct hypotheses that are possible explanations for the ambiguities we see in the world around us. As we explore these hypotheses or ideas, we also begin to examine the natural links between ideas over time and space. The connections we make between ideas impact what we think and do. We become engaged in designing our own personal worlds. We make of things what we will, not just because we prefer order to chaos, but because our minds demand that this be done. Working with whatever tools and experiences are at our disposal, we invent the possible—our current explanation of how the world works. We are forced to live with our invention until additional data become available to us which we can then use to invent new possibilities.

In the early 1900s, scientists thought that knowledge within the field of physics was complete. Then along came Einstein and other physicists who introduced quantum physics and a whole new understanding of the physical world came into existence. Stephen Hawking and others are now playing with ideas that introduce even newer possibilities to scientists' understandings about our world (Boslough, 1985). Scientists operate on their current theories (stories) of the world, keeping an eye open for new concepts that will change those theories (Rosen, 1984). Scientists assume that the different aspects of our universe are intentional, nonrandom, and together operate to create a unified meaning of the world. These assumptions cause them to actively search for that unity and to constantly test out new hypotheses.

We see these same assumptions in young children as they try to understand the world. They expect to understand and continuously test out their ideas. Their intentions as learners are obvious, for example, when a young child makes a line of marks on a card and reads those marks as a letter-like message. The child assumes that those marks have meaning specific to the context of letter writing. The child writes with purpose and intention (Harste, Woodward, & Burke, 1984).

So too, as teachers, we work with our students to create productive learning environments in our classrooms using our current understandings about learning. We operate as intentional learners, with purposes that make sense to us at that point in time. We must also, however, continue to look for the ambiguities which will change what we know and how we teach.

Life for us is a constant construction of purpose as we intentionally bring organization to our personal worlds. We cannot exist sanely without bringing some kind of organization to the unending stream of ideas and experiences we encounter. As we act with purpose and intention on what curiosity has brought to our attention, we make choices about which questions and ideas we will think more about. The realization that we have choices, that there are alternatives open to us as learners, allows us to develop a sense of ownership and responsibility about our learning. As teachers, the realization that we have choices in how we teach brings a sense of responsibility that is both frightening and freeing. Our intentions as learners and teachers now make a difference

My ideas have grown because when I get an idea, it gives me another idea and I keep revising that idea until I get it just like I want it so I can write about it.

Carl, Grade 3

Learning as an active and intentional search for meaning

in that classroom. We can no longer shove the total responsibility for intention off onto a program or an administrator.

Intentionality involves living in a continuous present which is always in touch with the past and the future. As we act with intention on the world, we make choices based on the larger perspective of how our present choice is tied to both the past and the future. Our ability as learners to make the connections that bring meaning and organization to our lives is dependent on being able to connect current events to our past experiences and to our expectations for the future. These connections between the present, past, and future are constantly being challenged and reinvented as we encounter new data. This new data comes from a world filled with other people who impact our learning.

Sociability As individual learners we actively seek relationships with others. Our emotional, intellectual, and physical well being is invested in others because it is as social beings that our world becomes multi-dimensional. We borrow others' experiences and understandings to extend our available collection of ways to know the world. As learners, we retain ownership of our learning by remaining in charge of the borrowing. Our voices as learners change as we borrow from others but we are the ones making the decisions about those changes. As we borrow, we transform our own understandings and develop new voices. Our new voices are still our own, however, and not external voices that those with greater power imposed on us.

Our ability to empathize with others provides our only opportunity to stand outside ourselves and observe who we are and what we are doing. These socially provided observation points lend flexibility to our personal worlds. They create choices that would not be available to us if we were isolated from others. We have potentials for learning that would never be realized without these social relationships.

Our personal world is extended and expanded to the

Before I never knew things needed to have meaning.

Alicia, Grade 3

The learner is in charge of changes in thinking and perspective.

You can't learn near as much when you're alone because then even if you do come up with lots of ideas you're not learning anything new. You need other people's ideas.

Kim, Grade 3

extent that we are able and willing to confer with others. We don't just live in a social world, that social world is already within us determining how we think. The ways in which we talk and interact with other people become internalized and change the ways we think (Vygotsky, 1978). When we are in learning environments that allow us to take full advantage of what others have to offer, to really interact and learn from those around us, we create new potentials for ways of thinking. Learning then involves being able to attend to the demonstrations being offered by other learners and to confer with others about our understandings of our world. We need learning environments where we can see others actively learning and can engage in many collaborative dialogues about our ideas and experiences.

Last weekend, I finished reading Bridge to Terabithia. I started thinking about the book. I had a literature circle in my head. One side of my brain said one thing about the story and then the other side said, "No. Wait a minute. What about this?"

David, Grade 3

Literature circles changed me in my eyesight and in my brain too.

Karen, Grade 3

The Natural Learner in Process When the learner's world is intact and when no outside force acts to constrain or circumvent the learner's use of curiosity, intentionality, and sociability, then these natural forces work together in powerful

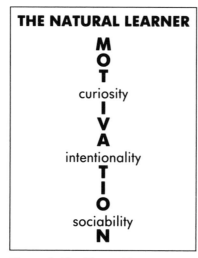

Figure 1. The Natural Learner

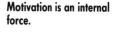
Motivation is an internal force.

I have made the biggest change that I ever have because I used to read because the teacher said to go and read. Now I read because I want to.

Kim, Grade 3

ways. Ambiguities are attended to, order is sought, and others become a social extension of ourselves. The learner is motivated. *Motivation* thus becomes a force internal to the natural learner and a result of the natural learning process being functionally intact rather than an external force applied to the learner by someone else (Figure 1).

When this natural learning process is allowed to function, there is never a question as to who is in charge. Learners have control of their own learning. They do not wait for someone else to tell them what to learn. Their questions, not someone else's, initiate and motivate the learning process. Because they are in charge, learners can change direction and develop new questions as they are engaged in the process of learning.

Think of one or two instances in which you or someone you know has experienced the curiosity, intentionality, and sociability of a natural learning engagement.

....

Learner Stories:

....

A Community of Learners

Well, last year the books had an influence on me. I didn't want to read them. They weren't any good.

Philip, Grade 3

While it is in the nature of people to learn, it is not the nature of all learning that it be productive. Awareness of this fact led Dewey (1938) to distinguish between miseducation and education. While miseducation might lead to the learning of new knowledge, it restricts the potential of future experiences. The new knowledge leads to a dead end, either because of the isolated nature of the knowledge or the negative impact of the learning experience on the learner. The learner may end up with an isolated skill or fact that is stored away but is so disconnected that the learner is unable to use it in further learning experiences—there is no transfer of knowledge because there are no connections. Or the learner may be involved in learning experiences that are stressful and negative. All of us have had experiences such as learning a new sport or how to use a piece of equipment that were so negative that we resolved never to become involved in that activity again. Statistics from the American Book Industry show that many adults actively choose not to read books once they leave school because of their negative school experiences with reading (Spiegel, 1981).

To be educative, a learning experience must not only generate fact, knowledge, or belief, it must also increase the likelihood that the learner will actually seek similar but expanded experiences in the future (Dewey, 1938). These educative experiences take place within a community of learners and are characterized by risktaking, reflection, and collaboration.

> Risktaking
> Reflection
> Collaboration

Risktaking Risk becomes an immediate result of a learner's curiosity. The ambiguities and experiences that the learner seeks naturally create alternative interpretations and therefore the possibility of wrong responses. Within any experience, we have to accept that there are alternative interpretations available concerning the physical characteristics of the actual situation, and the perceptions of other people who might be involved in that learning experience. Our world is an ambiguous one in which there are few right or wrong answers. To be a risktaker is to be willing to live with ambiguity and its consequences. We have to accept that in many situations there will never be right or wrong answers, only a series of possible answers.

Learning to live with ambiguity

Exploration naturally leads to choice and choice brings with it the potential to be wrong. Accepting the potential to be wrong or to never know if one is right or wrong is critical to the welfare of the learner because mistakes are a natural feature of all learning environments. To avoid risk means cutting off and putting limits on our curiosity as learners. It

I feel like Kino in The Big
Wave. *I am brave to say
something in front of the
class. Kino was brave to face
the big tidal wave like I am
brave to face the class.*

Brian, Grade 3

means accepting a passive role. Many engagements must simply be avoided and involvement in other engagements becomes dependent upon acceptance of some other learner's interpretations and solutions. Avoiding risk means becoming totally constrained by convention, by what others think is an acceptable response.

Risktaking is not something that learners either do or don't do in all situations. There are different factors that learners must consider in deciding what are acceptable risks. One such factor is the result of what we already know. Exploration of new ideas always operates on the edge of the known. Just past the boundaries of our currently comfortable beliefs is an area where we have some expectations but few certainties. When we or others insist upon the support of too much that is already known, this restricts the potential for new discoveries. We simply stay with what we already know and don't consider new possibilities. Many adults have failed to realize the potential uses for computers in their lives because they view computers as far removed from what they already know. In contrast, children often see computers as a natural part of their lives and willingly explore new possibilities for their use.

*The way I have grown as a
thinker is I used to think in
the wrong way like thinking
there is only one right
answer. But now I think there
is more than one answer.*

Lynn, Grade 3

Moving too far beyond the known, on the other hand, means the loss of context within which to organize and interpret our new findings. We cannot find the connections between the new findings and what we already know to make those understandings our own. The new insights remain floating out there somewhere, unconnected and therefore difficult to learn and easy to forget.

Our learning needs to both connect with and go beyond what is already known to us. Vygotsky (1978) conceived of this territory as the "zone of proximal development"—an area just beyond what we already know and where we can learn with the support of others. Learners need to build new knowledge and belief upon current understandings. As learners, we venture out into new territory but, to keep ourselves oriented, we always stay within sight of what we already know.

*In groups, I learn from what I
say and what others say. I
can learn from all my
classmates. The more we
help people, the more we
learn. I think learning
spreads around when we all
help people. It makes me
feel good when I know I am
learning.*

Crystal, Grade 3

Recognizing the demands of alternative situations is a second factor to consider in becoming an effective risktaker. We are less willing to predict in relation to the indecipherable word in our doctor's prescription than we are in the friendly letter from our old college roommate. We feel freer to substitute ingredients in a familiar recipe to avoid an additional trip to the store if we are not having guests come to dinner. As learners, we decide on the degree and kind of risk based on the particulars of the engagement or situation. When these decisions about risk are taken out of our hands, our learning is inhibited, especially when every context is presented by others as demanding high degrees of accuracy and a high cost for being wrong.

Immersing ourselves in a group of other risktakers is a third factor that impacts us as risktakers. Together we form a community, ready to receive others' thoughts and to share our own. We confer with each other, comparing and contrasting the options which the intentionality of individual members has made available to the group. The risks that each individual takes are cushioned by community membership and by the realization that others are also taking risks. Many teachers who have made changes in their classrooms have felt a need to be part of some type of teacher support group for this reason.

Finally, the boundaries of productive risktaking are expanded when we can try out our different predictions for solutions within the same experience or test our predictions across different situations. Composing is not stressful if we and others in our environment recognize the use of revisions and rough drafts and of collaboration with other authors as basic to the composing process. We have more confidence in our abilities as curriculum developers if we can test out new teaching ideas with more than one group or in more than one context before we determine whether or not they will work as we predicted. Simply put, knowing that we will have the opportunity to make changes in our ideas increases our willingness to take a risk and act as decision makers.

In literature circles, we support each other. Like if they cannot think of anything to say and they think it's hard for that person, they will not push that person, they will just try to help that person by asking other questions.

Nicole, Grade 3

In literature circles and authors' circles, people say what they think about the book and then other people can either agree or disagree.

Jason, Grade 3

This year I learned that you don't have to be a perfect person. You just need to be yourself.

Jamie, Grade 3

Because of the social nature of learning, situations of miseducation can arise. The outside forces impacting the learner can be coercive and thus restrictive. The coercion may take any of a variety of forms. It may involve the use of punishment, ridicule, or deprivation as a reaction to mistakes. It is an example of coercion to have to produce a second final copy of a paper to eliminate missed conventions such as misspellings, instead of being expected to use this knowledge in the final drafting of the next document which we author.

Outside force may involve others imposing an already determined "right" answer. We are not really being asked to learn, but simply to memorize the predigested judgments of someone else. A college course in which your essay on the effectiveness of supply side economics will not be warmly received unless it reflects the professor's position, even when there are competing authoritative positions on the issue, is an act of coercively limiting the learner's judgment.

The miseducative responses of learners to outside coercion are predictable. In degrees of increasing severity, we can decide to postpone, compromise, replace, abandon, or stop our own learning. We can attempt to postpone decisions, anticipating the departure of the coercive force. This response is often seen in classrooms where students "behave" only until the teacher leaves the room or where students read only when assigned materials. We can compromise our decisions by adding incompatible elements of the power person's beliefs into our beliefs. This compromise occurs in classrooms where teachers who believe in the holistic nature of learning and language accept the administrations' belief in the importance of standardized tests which measure use of fragmented pieces of language.

Another response to coercion is to totally replace our best judgments with the judgments of another person. We dismiss our own intuitions and beliefs as having any validity and accept the beliefs of someone else. Students who have had some type of "disabled learner" label placed on them often come to accept the view that adults have of them as learners and persons. Another possible response is to abandon any attempt to make sense and simply comply to the physical demands of the situation through memorized responses. Or, in final desperation, we can close down entirely as intentional beings trying to make sense of our world and stop both mental and physical participation. It seems safer to stop thinking and responding than to risk being considered wrong by those in power. If learners don't answer a teacher's question, their responses can't be judged as wrong. In many professions, this response is often seen as "burnout."

All learning is risky business. Those risks which are viewed as positive by people are frequently referred to as challenges. Along with Dewey (1938), we can simply call them education.

I was scared at the beginning. I didn't want to do anything. I was afraid I would do it wrong. I was afraid of the other kids. But now I'm just fine.

Pat, Grade 1

Reflection The challenges which we pursue as learners increase our awareness of our learning and the learning of others around us. As we act intentionally within a community of learners, we become increasingly aware that others are also acting with intentionality and are inventing their personal worlds. This recognition encourages us to observe the organizational web of others' decisions, both as a distinct whole and in contrast to our own organizational webs. Just as we are developing our own unified theories of how the world operates, so is everyone else around us. We "try on" their perspectives to understand how they view the world and how their views compare to ours.

As we borrow other points of view, we discover that we can mentally stand both inside and outside of an event at the same time. We suddenly realize that we can look at that event from both our own perspective and that of someone else. The realization that we can be in two places at once forms the basis for reflection.

Our ability to reflect is inhibited when we or others use an authority's perspective to shut off our view. When this occurs, we are forced to accept a single perspective which comes from outside of ourselves. Our ability to reflect is also

Learning to stand outside ourselves

inhibited if we are not in learning situations where we can observe and interact with other learners so that an outside perspective becomes available. When we are unable to interact with others, we are limited to an insider's perspective.

Reflection brings with it increased flexibility as a problem solver. We are more comfortable with our own risks as we become more aware of the reasoning behind those risks. We begin to see that even our mistakes possess an internal logic. We had a reason for doing what we did. Our mistakes reflect our thinking processes. Many of the current "self-help" books on the market are aimed at helping people think through why they continuously become involved in negative relationships. Once they understand their thinking processes, they have a better chance of forming productive relationships rather than continuing to make the same mistakes. The same issue is present for students who receive a page of math or statistics problems which are marked as incorrect. Unless students are encouraged to reflect on their reasoning behind their solutions and to share their problem solving strategies with each other, they have no way to improve their mathematical understandings.

As we reflect on the reasoning of others, we become more aware of the variety of logical solutions available in any one set of circumstances. We are more likely to continue our efforts when our own initial reasoning breaks down. We come to expect the availability of logical alternatives and are less likely to consider any problem incapable of solution or to stop our explorations with the discovery of one logical solution. We become capable of seeing beyond the surface variations of situations to recognize conceptual similarities and therefore the possibility that the logic of one situation will work in a second situation.

Reflection on what and how we are learning increases our ability to prioritize. Being capable of forming a mental picture of the workings of the process frees us to be selective and to make decisions concerning the weight and worth of individual parts of the process. The development of a cohesive

Sometimes the other people in my group have better ideas than my own. Then later when I am doing something by myself, I have more ideas.

Joanna, Grade 6

In math, we don't just want the answer because that can't help at all. We want how and what and why.

Carl, Grade 3

I have grown a lot in conferencing. I used to never conference but now I conference all the time. I like to conference because I know I can get more ideas from other stories for my own stories. I was conferencing with some other people and they noticed that I have a style of writing. I saw the style of writing, too. I was proud of myself for having a style. The style is this: I take some of my experiences and things I like to do and make a book out of it.

Adrian, Grade 3

mental picture of any process demands that we ignore less significant features in favor of capturing the broad outlines and key relationships of the process. Even with prioritizing, reflection still requires time to think. When we rush ahead or when others do not value thinking time, we lose the opportunity we need to reflect. As teachers, we often get so immersed in the daily "doing" of classroom life that we fail to find the time for ourselves and our students to think and reflect on that "doing." With the loss of reflection also comes the loss of control over change in our classrooms.

Reflection generates and supports our sense of authority concerning our engagements in the world. Being an authority does not make us reflective thinkers. Instead, being reflective thinkers in a community of other learners allows us to develop our own authority. We are in control of ourselves and of our intentions. We have a sense of our future because we have an understanding of our past.

Collaboration It is our growing awareness of the intentionality of others that supports the development of reflection. So, too, we are encouraged to develop our social nature into formal relationships by the recognition that supportive others can extend and expand the potential of our intellectual searches for questions and explanations. The social setting within which these relationships are formed has a major impact on the potentials and the constraints that any learner perceives for risktaking and reflection within a community of learners.

Because people are naturally social, they have developed many types of groups to serve a variety of needs. Some groups are very loosely knit and are brief in duration, such as the audiences we form to share a concert or ballgame. Some have specific functions, such as a homeowners group or a grocery co-op. The scope of some is broad and enduring, such as the family unit. Each group has a certain pattern of relationships that determines the actions between the individual and the group. Some groups may be marked by hierarchies of control

Before we did not look back on our learning. This year we look back on our learning and learn more. Before I got frustrated when I got something wrong. This year I don't because it is the learning that counts. This year we are more like a team than a class.

Julie, Grade 3

I like it that we aren't in groups of high, middle, and low. I already knew I was low. I needed someone smarter to push my own thinking.

Lark, Grade 6

I think teachers should try having kids work together because it can make their students smarter and it is fun for the kids so they want to do it. It can help the teacher learn too. I think working together helps the whole class.

Chris, Grade 3

Recognizing an enduring and shared commitment

When you work with others, it stretches your mind. You get more ideas. Like maybe your partner thinks of something you never would have and you think of something your partner wouldn't have.

Josh, Grade 2

We don't have levels of reading. We are all valued equally and our thinking is valued.

Darcy, Grade 3

and responsibility while others are marked by their use of compromise as their strategy for making decisions. The pattern of relationships that best seems to meet the needs and interests of a community of learners is that provided by the complex relationships of a collaborative.

Collaboratives are characterized by the ways in which members think and work together. They are initiated by the recognition of some shared commitment that is more general and lasting in nature than a simple goal or objective. The commitment is long range, enduring, and of general importance. While this shared commitment gives a sense of focus to the community of learners, it does not assume a specific end that all learners must reach.

The complex nature of the commitment calls forth the second feature of collaboratives, the valuing of diversity. The diverse talents, experiences, and perspectives of the group members increase and expand the resources that the group brings to learning far beyond the means of any single member within it. The individual is not subsumed to the group. Instead, the individual uniqueness of each member's contribution to the group is valued and is what allows the group to think together in productive ways. Members of the group do not just cooperate and work together, they actively listen and think together, trying to understand and make use of the diverse perspectives available in that group.

Member contributions are not evaluated on the basis of quantity. Because the unique member contributions are equally indispensable to the process, they are given equal value. Equal value means that all learners, no matter how apparently limited their experience or knowledge, come to recognize themselves and are recognized by the others, as competent contributors. Learners confer with each other. It is this two-way process of receiving and sharing with others that allows learners to become unique individuals. They become part of a generative and cohesive group of learners.

The competence of contributors is enhanced by the fact that the collaborative does not assign formal roles to individuals. Rather, roles are generated by the needs of the project and filled by individuals as they recognize the suitability of their available contribution to the project. Because people are not "type cast" there is greater likelihood that none of their talents or knowledge will go unused. Students can move in and out of the role of the teacher as they interact with others instead of that role being the "property" of the adult learner in that classroom. Individuals are seen in terms of their potentials, not in terms of their limitations.

The focus on potentials does not mean that members of a collaborative expect only and always to succeed in every project or task. On the contrary, membership in the collaborative offers the feature of shared vulnerability. The group cushions the mistakes which are part of all risktaking. Mistakes are valued for the cues which they provide concerning the processes that are currently the focus of the members' curiosity. The group recognizes that new knowledge is produced even if there is not an immediate resolution to the current problem. No individual members, however, are ever forced to put themselves so far away from their past experiences that they become vulnerable to ridicule or disconnected from their own intentions.

This need for a collaborative group to support risktaking has led many teachers to form study groups with other educators. In these groups, teachers can share and support each other as well as critically think through problems and issues. These groups give teachers a context for controlling their own change in their classrooms instead of mandating change that is too far beyond their current understandings.

Because the focus of collaboratives is on inquiry and not on final solutions, consensus becomes the key process for developing understanding into new knowledge. Concensus decisions demand the use of all the features of collaboratives—common commitment, valued diversity, equal value of contributions, fluid roles, and shared vulnerability. Individual knowledge, experience, and understanding become a pooled resource as members confer on any question.

You can do better things when you work together because if you're doing a poster maybe you can't draw but your partner can so your project turns out better.

Wrennie, Grade 6

In this room everybody is a teacher and a learner. Last year, there was just one teacher and 24 kids.

Michael, Grade 3

Here everybody is equal. We can all read books and talk about them with each other. Some people might take longer to read a book but everybody does it and everybody has something to say.

Jamie, Grade 3

Everyone has a chance to give their opinion and even if you don't agree with that person, you keep on talking because you know that you will get more ideas. You aren't trying to figure out one right answer. In reading groups, when someone gave the right answer, we were done talking. In literature circles, we keep on going. We try to come up with as many different directions as possible.

Chris, Grade 3

Inviting new learning opportunities within the community

I think working with a group of people helps you get along with other people. You can get a lot of ideas out of listening to the other people. When talking to other people in a group, you feel like you CAN say things, and you CAN talk. When you are with yourself, you can't get new ideas from other people. Being in groups changed my learning because I can learn from the other people and they can learn from me.

Lori, Grade 6

In contrast to employing authority or compromise to make decisions, concensus involves exploring the diverse perspectives available within the group without creating winning and losing sides. The dialogue is brisk, challenging, wide-ranging, and conducted in depth, but it is never coercive. Ideas, not members, are challenged, and individuals are not coerced into changing their points of view. When these parameters are in place, a community of learners will create knowledge and understanding through concensus that go beyond the current abilities of any individual member. The new knowledge, in turn, will create new meanings and new potential risks.

The Community of Learners in Process The new potential risks created out of the concensus process serve as invitations to members to develop new intentions. As learners become secure and value their own meaning making, they are more capable of supporting the meaning making of others. Learners become active at offering learning opportunities to others. Just as motivation can be seen as the internal force supporting the natural learner, *invitations* are the generative force propelling a community of learners forward (Figure 2). Dewey's criteria for measuring the educative process has been fulfilled. The force of the present learning experience has acted to increase the likelihood that the learners will seek related future experiences. The current experience invites the next. Education is generative.

Think of one or two instances in which you have experienced the risktaking and reflection of a collaborative experience.

. . . .

Learner Stories:

. . . .

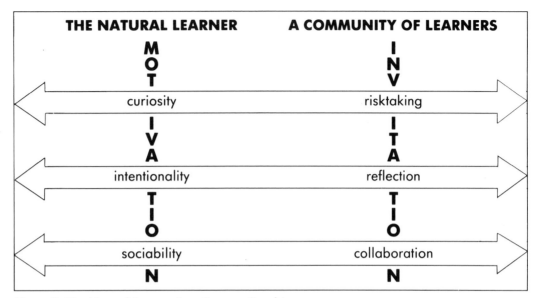

Figure 2. The Natural Learner in a Community of Learners

The Collected Learner

Learning acts to throw learners off balance. The ambiguities that learners investigate with intent are threats to their current sets of beliefs. They feel out of balance because their world view is threatened. As part of the learning process, there must be periodic attempts to regain control, to re-establish equilibrium. Learners must mentally re-gather their forces and collect themselves when they find themselves facing ideas that do not fit in with their current beliefs.

Collected learners have a working hypothesis. This hypothesis constitutes their current world view. It will be the base upon which they will operate when they explore the next ambiguity that their curiosity raises. Learners' worlds are never at rest. They have to accept that there are no final solutions, only current best solutions. Collecting one's self becomes an aspect of the cycle that we call learning. This act of re-establishing equilibrium, of re-collecting one's self is characterized by tension, reflexivity, and connected knowing.

Well I think working together helps me as a reader because I can ask people what they think and see if I agree.

Tara, Grade 3

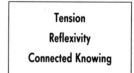

Tension There is always tension in learning because the act of learning itself reminds us that knowledge is tentative. The next act of learning could be the instigator for a major overhaul of our belief system. This tension is what keeps us alert, monitoring the possibilities, taking new risks, stretching ourselves and our capabilities. It is a positive force, a minimal electrical current that runs through our efforts, giving them life. Young children are continuously driven by this tension. Their understandings of language constantly change as they try out various ways of using language to communicate to others. Their predictions about the use of plurals is challenged when they realize that the plural of mouse is mice, not mouses.

Tension as a positive force in monitoring potentials

While tension is internal and natural to the learning process, outside forces can also act upon the learner. If these forces act to attack learners' intentionality or to ridicule their reflections, stress is created in the learning environment. This stress will encourage learners to close down investigation and will distract them from their intentionality. They lose sight of their own purposes for engaging in learning. While tension is the driving force that keeps learners moving ahead, stress leads to shutting off further learning experiences. When adults laugh at young children's ideas or creative uses of language, they can discourage further exploration of language.

The tension internal to the learning process encourages learners to establish a macro view of their efforts. It encourages them to seek mental distance in order to gain a holistic perspective. It helps ensure that they will not get bogged down with bits and pieces and lose sight of the overall picture. As learners pull themselves together from dealing with one question, they gather the broader perspective they need to make the next venture into curiosity. Each time they pull themselves together, they will bring a slightly different perspective to their next learning experience.

In our class, everything changes. All the work we do in here changes you slowly.

Jason, Grade 3

Carolyn discovered this tension and change in belief systems in a powerful way during her work on her master's degree. Her teaching experiences in a Reading Readiness class with African American children from a lower socioeconomic community had led her to pursue a master's degree in reading.

> It was only at the end of my master's program, when all I had to complete was my master's thesis that E. Brooks Smith and Kenneth Goodman joined the faculty at Wayne State University. Smith, who became my advisor, persuaded me to take a structural linguistics course from the English department and to take a graduate seminar on the reading process from Ken Goodman. These two experiences proved the major turning point in my professional life. My view of language as a static 'to be learned' convention was shattered. I had my first glimpse of language as a fluid thinking process. (Short, 1986)

Because of this experience, Carolyn became involved in miscue research with Ken and developed many new questions about reading as a linguistic process. Later research experiences created tensions that led her to ask questions about language as a social process and as a semiotic sign system. Each experience raised questions which she explored and the answers to those questions changed her view of language and led to new questions.

Reflexivity Because tension acts to maintain learners' perspectives, it also acts to encourage us to take a reflexive, long-distance stance in regard to our knowing. While we have been reflective—attempting to explain ourselves to ourselves or to others on the basis of a specific experience—we begin to step back even more and to seek more generalized understanding and knowledge. We are encouraged to explore the potential our current knowledge has for solving problems other than the one which has been the object of our immediate investigation. We are no longer in the immediate crisis of solving the problem but have reached a working solution and so can now mentally step further back. For example, readers can move from reflecting on the strategies they used to read and think through a specific mystery novel to stepping back and thinking about how these strategies can be used more broadly as they read from other texts.

Because I accept everyone in my class, it is easier to understand and accept people in the world for their differences.

Miranda, Grade 3

I didn't used to know what to do when I came to something I didn't know. Then I read with you and you said to skip it and go on. I tried it and it worked in that story. Now when I read, I try different things when I come to something I don't know. One thing I do is skip it and read on and then say "Now I know it" just like I did with you.

Erin, Grade 1

Formalizing the knowledge gained from immediate experience to make it available to future experiences

Children who serve as class editors for a week or two often undergo a change in perspective about the importance of conventions such as spelling for readers. They bring a different perspective to their own writing because of their experiences as an outside reader of others' writing. These experiences help them realize that outside readers need spelling and other conventions to create meaning from a story even though the writer does not. The chance to step back and consider conventions for a period of time gives them the opportunity to broaden their understanding about the role of conventions.

Our knowledge becomes more formalized and abstracted from the immediate circumstances and thus more available for general use. We are better able to see below the surface features to the organizing structures that support those features. As we see these underlying patterns, we can make judgments concerning similarities, differences, and relationships among these patterns. From these connections, we can develop broad frames of reference that will impact the questions and predictions we will make in future experiences.

Connected Knowing Our judgments as learners about underlying patterns become part of our process of recasting and adjusting personal world views. We collect ourselves, regather our forces, make new connections, and establish a new equilibrium, a new balance of beliefs. We have control over our own connected knowing.

Creating a story out of our experience

Learners are, in a sense, storytellers (Rosen, 1984). The stories that we tell are a result of the intentionalities that we have pursued, the interpretations that we have given to our experiences, and the dialogues we have engaged in with other learners. We construct stories about our experiences as we dialogue with others and make connections between aspects of our current experience and stories we already have constructed from earlier experiences. Our view of the world becomes a web of interconnected stories which continues to grow and change in complexity. The stories reflect our authoritative world view and are the means by which we make our understandings and knowledge open to collaboration with intentional others.

As learners, we integrate our own personal knowledge with what we learn from others by developing the capacity to really listen and talk with others while continuing to speak and listen to ourselves. We constantly search for connections between what we already know and what we are currently experiencing in order to construct our own understandings or stories. Knowledge for us is always constructed and we recognize the temporary nature of what we know and that the knower is always an intimate part of the known. We examine, question, and develop our systems to use in constructing knowledge through our interactions with others. We do not depend on authorities to provide us with our answers or with the questions and the procedures to get the answers. We pursue our own questions and answers with the support of other learners to find the connections that make our world meaningful and our thinking productive.

The Collected Learner in Process Learners' stories empower collaborative relationships. At the same time that learners' stories enable them to recognize their own authority, they aid them in recognizing the storytelling authority of others. It is through the stories that learners tell each other that the option of alternative perspectives becomes available, that these options may be critically evaluated, and that we as learners come to see ourselves as empowered to act upon the world.

The invitations that learners offer to each other create personally authored stories. Learners do not just transfer others' stories into their own knowing, they transform others' stories and make them their own. They live in an intertextual world. *Empowered* learners act with authority. They become authors of their own lives (Figure 3). It is the consideration for this authorship which must form the basis of our curriculum planning.

The most important thing about first grade is that I got to know everybody and I got to make my own stories.

Adrienne, Grade 1

Last year, the teacher was in charge of everything but in this class, we are all in charge of ourselves.

Darcy, Grade 3

Through authorship, learners are empowered to act upon the world.

I've changed because now I say what I want to say and not what the teacher wants me to say.

Megan, Grade 3

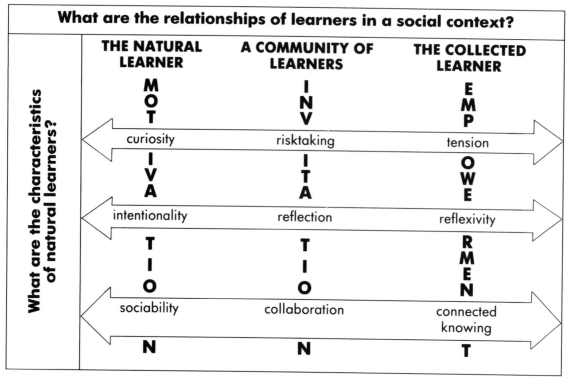

Figure 3. Understanding Curriculum as a Social Learning Process

Think of one or two instances in which your experience has resolved itself into a new and personally powerful understanding of the world.

....

Learner Stories:

....

An Authoring Cycle Model of Curriculum

A curriculum is a prediction concerning how people learn, what people should be learning, and the contexts that will support that learning. It is an organizational device intended to put the answers to those predictions into operation and to establish a context for future decisions. A curriculum is a reflection of the curriculum makers' learning theories and their best current understandings of the processes that define various fields of study. It must be metaphorically written in pencil and adjusted in response to the unexpected and the unpredicted. A curriculum always operates in the present by interpreting the past and predicting the future.

Our past experiences and our current set of understandings come together to create classroom and content structures which we intuitively prefer. We make decisions on the basis of what feels right and comfortable to us. This *intuitive curriculum* forms the data out of which we generate our reflective curricula—paper, enacted, and envisioned.

A curriculum is such a complex set of processes that its preservation on paper serves as a necessary external memory —a history of our thoughts. This *paper curriculum* allows us to apply, reflect, and adjust this set of processes as we are involved in classroom life. The *enacted curriculum* is composed of the actual learning engagements. As students and teachers participate in learning engagements, tensions arise out of unfulfilled needs. This disequalibrium signals a needed adjustment to our paper curriculum and leads to an envisionment of a potential new curriculum. For some span of

Paper
Enacted
Envisioned

time, this experience will be an "in-head" phenomenon, a cognitive and affective knowing which we are not yet able to articulate. This unarticulated awareness will formulate the *envisioned curriculum*. Our envisionments will be realized in an adjusted paper curriculum and the cycle will be renewed.

When we theorize, we have the luxury of momentarily freezing the process which we are studying and separating it into its components parts and functions for the purpose of analysis. The result of that analysis is a curriculum, a clarified model of our interpretations of that process with all of the key relationships and components assembled and working in accord. While our theories provide the underlying assumptions of the curriculum, our theoretical categories are not directly realized in the functions of that curriculum. There is always an abductive leap involved in how these theories are actually translated into a curriculum model in a classroom.

In the first secion of this book, we developed a theory of learning which we see as the basis of how we think about curriculum. In this section, we will present one example of a curricular model which is based on that theory. This model of curriculum, called the Authoring Cycle, is reflective of our belief that empowered learners become authors of their own lives.

Figure 4 identifies major components in the Authoring Cycle. We will discuss these components briefly and give some specific examples of related curricular strategies which we have been using in college, secondary, and elementary classrooms. Further information on the Authoring Cycle and the specific curricular strategies described in this section can be found in *Creating Classrooms for Authors: Reading-Writing Connections* (Harste & Short, with Burke, 1988).

Life Experiences

What has already happened to us is our invitation to the future. The knowledge and understanding that students already have about life come from the social and cultural com-

There's no waiting for the class or the teacher to come in. We can get right to work because we know the cycle of learning.

Steven, Grade 3

Experiences are what happens to you. Sometimes you want to write these ideas down to remember your life. You can write these ideas as stories or just entries in your reflection logs. Sometimes your past experiences help you choose books to read. It is fun to have the same experiences as the character in a book. It is also fun to share your experiences with someone else. This helps you get to know you classmates better.

Derek, Grade 3

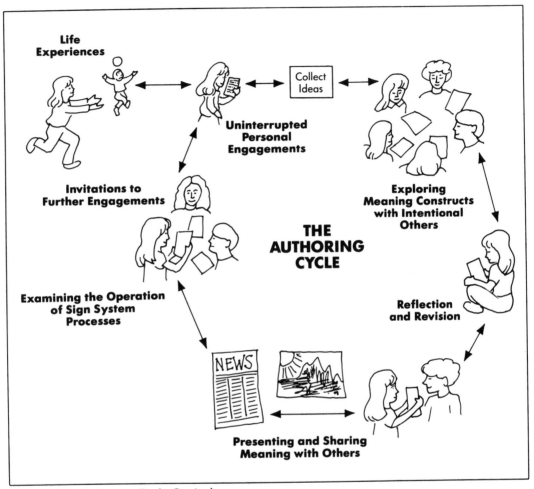

Figure 4. The Authoring Cycle Curriculum.

munities in which they live and learn both inside and outside of school. These understandings form the platform upon which they currently stand and from which they will launch themselves into the future. The curriculum then must always be connected to as well as go forward from students' life experiences. It is propelled by the participants' growing awareness of their own and others' experiences. What stu-

What we currently know is our invitation to the future

When the class interviews me, I look at myself in a different way. I feel important. I think as I study about other people, they become important like I am. I have learned how people are special and important.

Candice, Grade 3

I was worried when I came to third grade because I didn't know anyone in the class. We interviewed each other and put together a newspaper so we could learn about everyone in the room. We worked in small groups and in partners. So that I soon knew everyone in the room.

Katherine, Grade 3

In first grade, the teacher told me what to write about and after I got that book done, I was not proud of it. But now we can write whatever we want to and when I am done with all my books, I am proud of them. They are me.

Nicole, Grade 3

dents know is the touchstone upon which curriculum will be negotiated.

One curricular strategy which connects to students' life experiences is called *Getting to Know You*. Getting to Know You involves students pairing off to interview each other concerning either their personal or professional lives. Whether the interviewers are children or college students, their purpose is to interview another person to get to know them better and to introduce that person to the rest of the group. Students are given a chance to share orally from their interviews. The interviews then become an initiating experience for the Authoring Cycle. In the succeeding days, group members use their interview notes to write a rough draft, take the draft to Authors Circle, revise and edit the draft, and publish a newspaper that introduces the group to themselves and to interested others such as parents and visitors.

A second example is *Family Stories* which involve students in collecting the "remember when" stories that people always reminisce about at family gatherings. Students interview family members about these stories and bring their notes to share the stories orally with others. These stories then move through the Authoring Cycle to be published in a newspaper or book. As students collect these stories, they come to understand their family communities in a different way.

Whenever students are involved in experiences where they have choices, there is a greater likelihood that they will be able to make choices that allow them to connect with what they already know. Readers need choices in what they read and in how they respond to that reading just as writers need choices in topics, media, and interpretation. Units of study are more productive when they begin with students brainstorming what they already know and what they want to know more about in relation to that topic. In uninterrupted engagements with meaning, the focus is on classroom structures and activities that are open and allow learners at all levels of knowledge and proficiency to connect, in their own way, with those engagements.

....

What are 2 or 3 experiences in your life which have had great impact on you?

....

Uninterrupted Personal Engagements

We learn through doing, through actually engaging in learning for particular purposes. There are two bases on which uninterrupted personal engagements become the initiating function for the Authoring Cycle. The first deals with the nature of communication and the other concerns the nature of learning.

Sign systems (i.e., language, art, music, mathematics, dance) serve two coordinated functions. They are the devices that we use to create and explore meaning and through which we share and revise meaning. In natural environments, aspects of multiple communication systems are employed together. We talk, write, and draw at the same time. Rarely does an event involve the construction of meaning through only one system. The more complex the understandings or knowledge, the more likely it is that multiple systems will be used to communicate those understandings to others.

Motivation to engage in uninterrupted learning experiences is an internal function of learners. The curious, intentional, and social nature of learners operates within their life experiences to motivate and focus their interests. Because their new knowledge must be based upon their understandings, learners must already be engaged in the act of learning *before* curricular invitations can be generative of new learning. Learners cannot learn what we invite them to learn if they are disconnected from their world of knowing. Our task as teachers becomes how to create classroom settings that immerse students in learning experiences based on their past

Dancing helped me be like a character in a book. I learned to stop killing my characters in my writing.

Clyde, Grade 3

Music helps me think out my thoughts.

Maria, Grade 2

Learners must be connected to their own personal known world.

*hen you
e chosen
lso do
piuys wiin costumes or
puppets. You can read with
your friends or read alone.
Wide reading is a time to
read picture books and
chapter books. It is important
for readers to have time to
be able to just take time to
read and play with being
readers.*

Marita, Grade 3

*I hear music in my mind
when I read. I look at the
cover and find a song in my
head to match it.*

Anna, Grade 2

*You can write what you want.
But it must have meaning to
it. I collect tidbits of what I
see and hear.*

Audrey, Grade 3

experiences and that we can then use to invite them to consider new learning opportunities. Instead of reading books whose purpose is to teach reading, we want our students to read literature and informational books as well as menus, directions, and maps where their purpose is to experience and learn something important to them. Instead of filling in blanks on workbook pages and writing about creative writing topics for the teacher, we want our students writing pen pal letters, messages, journals, learning logs, stories, poems, and articles for many different audiences. We want students to have the opportunity to author in other communication systems such as art, music, drama, and mathematics. They need many uninterrupted "doing" experiences for purposes that are meaningful to them as learners.

Authors Folders are personal folders where authors preserve ideas for future pieces of writing, drafts, and portions of draft documents. The writing in the folders is initially private and results from authors having large chunks of time available to write about topics important to their lives. These chunks of time have given students the opportunity to learn about the writing process through engaging in that process. They have been given invitations by class members that are options they might choose in their writing or they choose to pursue their own ideas.

Authors must decide which documents will remain private and which will be shared with others by moving them through the Authoring Cycle to be reconsidered in terms of a broader audience. The documents in the folders are dated so that authors can periodically reflect on the history of their thoughts and writing flexibility by looking through their folders.

Shared Reading involves readers in a collaborative oral reading experience where a lead reader reads a familiar picture book or Big Book to the class while the class reads/recites as much of the text as they know or can predict. In **Readers Theatre**, character and narrator parts are assigned to individual readers. Readers each highlight the parts that they will read aloud and then, without further preparation, the participants give a reading of the story. Both experiences give readers the opportunity to engage in oral reading for purposes that make sense to the reader and to learn about reading through reading.

Drawing Conversations engage two learners in a conversation through drawing. The two share one piece of paper and pencil. One begins drawing and then hands the pencil to the other artist who continues the drawing. No talking is allowed. All communication is through the drawing.

Other uninterrupted experiences in art might involve providing students with media such as watercolors or pastels and giving them a chance to experiment in creating a picture on a topic of importance to them. As with writing, some of these pictures remain private while others might be touched up or revised to share with others. In all uninterrupted experiences, the focus is on learners becoming involved in exploring that process as a way to create meaning for themselves. Some of what they create, they will share and explore further with others. In all cases, learners need large blocks of time to explore, a wide range of materials to use in their explorations, and the opportunity to explore these materials for purposes that are "real" or meaningful to them personally.

With art, I can show a lot at one time. I can get it all out at the same time. I get a lot more details than when I write. It shows the picture in my mind.

Patrick, Grade 2

I have changed as an artist because now I try to communicate my feelings through illustrating. Before I just drew to make the book prettier.

Carl, Grade 3

. . . .

What are 2 or 3 topics which interest you and about which you have questions?

. . . .

Exploring Meaning Constructs With Collaborative Others

It is in talking with others that we begin to be able to hear ourselves and to consider other perspectives. As we recognize our reader needs in reacting to another author, we begin to be able to plan for other readers' needs in reacting

Literature circles take the ideas out of your head rather than keeping all the ideas in your head.

Jamie, Grade 3

to our own authoring. We understand and develop our own thinking through trying to explain it to someone else and we consider new perspectives through listening and building from what others have to say. When we talk with others about what we have read or written or drawn, we learn to step outside the process and take a more analytical perspective. We are able to think through our "rough draft" ideas with others instead of being forced into immediately having to produce final draft thinking.

Authors' Circles consist of a small group of authors who all have a work of writing in progress. After each author reads a piece of writing aloud to the group, the others respond by sharing what they heard, asking questions about meaning, and indicating particularly effective or confusing parts of the piece. Authors come to Authors' Circle when they have a piece of writing they want to think more about with other people.

Literature Circles play the same function in reading. A small group of readers who have all read the same piece of literature gather together to explore their "rough draft" (in process) understandings of that literature. In Text Set discussions, each reader reads a different but related book so that when the group gets together they focus on comparisons and personal connections across their books. In both types of literature groups, the small group discussions focus on multiple interpretations and connections. Just as readers and writers explore their texts with others, artists or actors can explore with others the meanings they have constructed through art and drama to examine what those meaning constructs are communicating to others.

Mathematical Circles occur as students work through mathematical stories individually and then meet together as a small group to share and compare their strategies for mathematically thinking through possible solutions to that story.

In **Paired Books**, two books that are related to each other but present different perspectives are put together. Two readers share the reading of the books and then discuss the ways in which the two books are similar and/or different. They then try to find a way to show the comparisons between the two books using some type of chart or picture or other graphic form.

Exploring our meaning constructions with collaborative others gives all of us the chance to feel that others have really listened and responded to the stories we have to tell through art, drama, and writing. These collaborative circles facilitate growth by capitalizing on the social nature of learning and authoring. We learn because we are part of a collaborative group who think together and expand each other's current ideas and perspectives.

In math, we work in groups. We do experiments to know what it means and to understand it. Not to just find the answer.

Barbara, Grade 3

In literature circles, you get to know the person better and how that book relates to their life and you and them relate.

Jamie, Grade 3

In this room, we work together and share what we know. That way everyone knows more in the end.

Carl, Grade 3

....

When have you collaborated successfully with another person on an important project?

....

Reflection And Revision

Once we have had an opportunity to explore our meaning constructs with others, we need the chance to reflect on the suggestions and comments that have been raised. We are now better able to take a spectator stance to our meaning constructs. We see them with different eyes because we are able to distance ourselves from our efforts and to reflect on the relationship between our intentions and our production. This reflection leads to decisions about whether and how we will revise those constructions.

Authors are in charge of their own productions.

In writing and drawing, students may add or delete or modify some part of their piece. In reading, students may change their interpretations of the stories they have read. Because learners are in charge of making these changes, their

Some of the ways I revise is that I take words and add them. Sometimes I even have to get rid of words, sentences, etc. Because the main idea fades away and the sentence would not make sense.

Jason, Grade 3

voices as learners remain their own even as they are trans-
formed by their social experiences.

....

What are some instances in which time and social experience have acted to change your beliefs or assumptions
about something?

....

Presenting and Sharing Meaning With Others

When we decide that we want to publicly share the meanings
that we have constructed through art, music, drama, or language with others, we need the perspective of an outside critic
or editor. We can never divorce ourselves entirely from our
own communication. Authors tend to read what they mean
when they examine their own texts so meaning constructs
which will become formal and public need the collaborative
attentions of other persons. Going public and formal involves
additional effort.

Authors must first discern a powerful functional need to
go public. There must be a real meaning making and sharing
need to reach people beyond those who have acted as collaborators during the composing of the text. The form and
format of any publication of meaning must be suited to its
purposes and must be based on use. Letters get delivered,
newspapers get distributed, books are kept available for re-
peated and varied use, murals are displayed in areas where
they are easily viewed, and dramas are presented to audiences.
The original decision to go public needs to be a functional
one. There has to have been a learner perceived need or purpose. Many meaning constructs never become formal but are
kept informal and/or private. Only a small percentage of the
meanings we construct go on to be formally published.

*When I publish, I can either
hand write my story or type it
on the computer. Some other
things we publish are
magazines, poems, sports,
articles, newspapers,
biographies, research
projects, and games. We can
publish anything someone
else would want to read.*

Alicia, Grade 3

When we come into contact with our prospective audience, we encounter the function of socially established conventions. As long as writing is directed toward ourselves, it need only be functional. Much can go unstated, spellings may be invented, and redundant cues such as capitalization, punctuation, and spacing may be disregarded. As long as we can read what it says, the piece is functional. However, when we want to share our knowledge and interests with others, we begin to see that conventions function to support our audience. Conventional spellings exist to support the reader, not the writer.

Conventions make our thoughts accessible to others.

In writing, **Editors' Table** plays this function for authors who want to publish their work. Each week, a small group of students takes a turn serving in the role of newspaper or book editors. The editors establish the editing codes they will use to deal with both the sense and the conventions of the document. Each succeeding group of editors revises these editing codes and procedures so that a history of editing is built up in that classroom. Once the piece is edited, it is typed and illustrated by the author who shares the finished book with the class in a time of celebration.

I have changed in editing because now I use capital letters at the right places. I used to use them at the wrong places or not at all. Reading other people's stories helped me figure out how to do this.

Carl, Grade 3

Another form of celebration and publication takes place when students in a literature group decide they want to make a formal presentation to the class. The group thinks about what they want to communicate in relation to their discussion of the literature they read. They then put together a formal presentation to convey the most important concepts. Their presentations might be a piece of writing, a mural, a class discussion, or a skit. After sharing their presentation, the class has an opportunity to "receive" the presentation by telling the group what they enjoyed about it and asking further questions.

Walking Journals are reflective documents that focus on a topic or area of concern to the participants. The journal is begun by writing the initiating thought on the first page and then is passed around from person to person with each person reading the previous comments and adding her or his own.

These journals serve a public informal function and so never go to editing or formal publication. **Classroom Newspapers,** in contrast, are regularly scheduled public publications that serve as outlets for student, teacher, and parent writing.

When learners publicly present the meanings they have constructed to others, they experience the satisfaction of successfully communicating with an audience. The thrill they experience as they present their work to others encourages them to continue in other uninterrupted engagements, to continue authoring through writing, art, mathematics, music, and drama. It also encourages others to make their own attempts to author meaning.

Yippie! That's what I say when I am an author.

Candice, Grade 3

....

Describe some times when you have "gone public" with your meaning.

....

Examining The Operation of Sign System Processes

I go back and look at my stories and see if they make sense. If they don't make sense, I know I have trouble.

Michael, Grade 1

As learners engage, explore, and present their understandings, they are constantly stretching the current limits of their learning strategies and functional uses of sign systems. In this way, they create a personal need for new knowledge about the processes that they are using. This need is met through strategy instruction. The teacher or another student organizes an experience to highlight the stated needs and invites the concerned learners to examine those sign system operations. These are reflective moments in which learners purposefully investigate the process and in which some aspect of that sign system is highlighted for reflection.

Reflection generates strategy instruction.

Examples of some strategy lessons related to reading include *Pre-Reading, Synonym Substitution,* and *Schema Stories* (Goodman & Burke, 1984). Pre-Reading is a strategy which focuses on having students read the title, look at pictures and graphs, slowly run a finger down the entire text, and then share what they think the text might be about before they actually read it. Synonym Substitution involves taking a passage and replacing underlined words or phrases with a synonym. As the group orally reads through the passage, students can read anything that makes sense as they reach an underlined word or phrase. Schema Stories involve cutting a text into key text segments and having students assemble the story by reading the segments aloud to decide on an appropriate sequence.

Each of these strategy lessons highlights a particular aspect of the reading process but does so by having students read and discuss a whole text with other readers. Students can also offer strategy lessons to each other. The child who figures out how to handle unknown character names during reading or how to add suspense to their writing can offer a strategy lesson to other interested students. Strategy lessons allow learners to take a step back and reflect on what they know about language and how they might use these understandings in future experiences.

> *I read to my teacher and ask her when I don't understand something. I skip a word and then go back and read it. If I don't remember the story, I reread it. I get the right point and I remember it in my head. Then I go and say, "What's this story about?" in my head. In a book, it says about a dog that ran away. I think about my dog. He ran away too.*
>
> *Sherri, Grade 1*

. . . .

List some strategies that you know you regularly use as a language (math, art, music, dance) user. List any ways in which you would like to improve as a language (math, art, music, dance) user.

. . . .

Invitations to Further Engagements

The cycle renews itself by the offering of new invitations that continue to move learners through the cycle. These invitations allow all students, including non-mainstream students, to use their language and experience as they engage in authoring and exploring with others. As learners are involved

> *This year we are all teachers and learners together meaning that the teacher gives us ideas and we give the teacher ideas.*
>
> *Darcy, Grade 3*

Each learner is responsible to contribute to the realization of the curriculum.

in authoring, they are able to express some of their intentions, but they also create new potentials for meaning for themselves and for others in that classroom. Each member of the community is responsible for contributing to the realization of the curriculum.

Collaborative Plans are a regularly scheduled segment of the day when individual and small group experiences are occurring. The students as well as the teacher list what they will do during this time period on a planning sheet and indicate whether they are inviting others to join them. **Action Research** involves group projects where each member of the group pursues an informal research question such as the type of cars their parents drive or where they can find print in their homes. Each member collects data and brings it to share with the others in Researcher Circles.

These invitations are options learners can choose to try out. They are not something they must do. They serve the function of keeping the authoring process continuously in motion. The curriculum strategies shared in this section highlight the Authoring Cycle as a general process framework that teachers and students can use to guide their own learning and to make productive decisions about curricular issues rather than seeking a specific set of activities.

. . . .

What are some current interests you would be prepared to invite others to explore with you?

. . . .

The Authoring Cycle in Action

The previous section on the Authoring Cycle highlights the variety of curricular strategies that can be part of this cycle and provides a better understanding of the role of each component. The danger of this description is that it can be seen as supporting an activity model of curriculum, a "grab bag" of great activities from which teachers can randomly choose each day. What is lost in this description is how this cycle becomes a framework for teachers and students as they structure their day and work over time. In this section, we want to describe a specific classroom setting where the Authoring Cycle provided an organizing framework for creating and organizing classroom experiences.

The authoring cycle as a framework for creating and organizing classroom experiences.

I think I can work better in this room because I can understand what I have to do without a workbook or being told by the teacher. The reason I know what to do is because we went through the reading and writing cycle at the beginning of the year and I can remember it.

Michael, Grade 3

The experience we want to share comes from a first grade classroom where Kathy was involved in a year-long collaborative study with Gloria Kauffman (Short, 1986). In March, the class became involved in a focused study on family and family relationships. The choice of topic grew out of a number of factors. One was the interests and needs of the children at that time. Issues related to families had been coming up frequently in class discussions and the children seemed to need time to really focus on understanding themselves in relation to their various family situations. Another factor was that the focus on family allowed Kathy and Gloria to introduce children to research strategies in a study where the research occurred through interviewing people rather than reading books. They were concerned that children develop a range of strategies for research rather than resorting to the "copy out of the encyclopedia" reports that so many older children write. In this particular school, all of the first grade classes took a trip to the zoo at the end of the school year and the children would be researching different animals through books and observation at the zoo. Researching families was a way to begin using research strategies with topics closer to children's own experiences. A final factor was that family was one of the units listed as first grade curriculum by the school.

The class began the unit by brainstorming as individuals and then as a whole class on "What is a family?" and "How do I fit within my family?" These two broad questions continued to serve as the focusing questions for the study throughout the next month. In the initial brainstorming, several children shared stories which we came to call "Remember When" stories. These are the stories that family members tell each other about "when you were little and did so and so." Kathy brought in several published family stories such as *The Relatives Came* (Rylant, 1985) and read them to the class. The growing interest in family stories became a major research project. The children interviewed family members about these "Remember When" stories and then brought their notes written on small pieces of paper to school. Each morning, the class gathered together for their group meeting and anyone who had a new story orally shared that story with the class. Often stories told by one child helped other children remember additional stories about their own families.

In writing, I can get my feelings out. I can write about my real life experiences.

Lark, Grade 6

Authoring through storytelling and writing

After several weeks of orally sharing their stories with the class, some of the children began to take their notes and write rough drafts of several of the stories they had shared. Soon everyone in the class was involved in writing up at least one of their stories. Most of the children took several of their stories through the Authoring Cycle as they wrote, conferenced, revised, edited, and then published collections of their family stories which became part of the classroom library. During this process, children decided that some of their stories were not appropriate to share with a broader audience or were stories they might write later. They made different decisions about whether to write and which of their stories, if any, they wanted to publish for others to read. At several points during this experience, the class met to discuss research strategies such as interviewing techniques, notetaking, and ways to share research with others.

Their family members were interested in these stories so the class decided to put together a newspaper containing a story from each class member, including the teachers. Gloria and Kathy had been gathering and sharing their own family stories along with the children. Each person chose one favorite story and the stories were put together into a newspaper that went home (Figure 5).

As the children collected and shared their own family

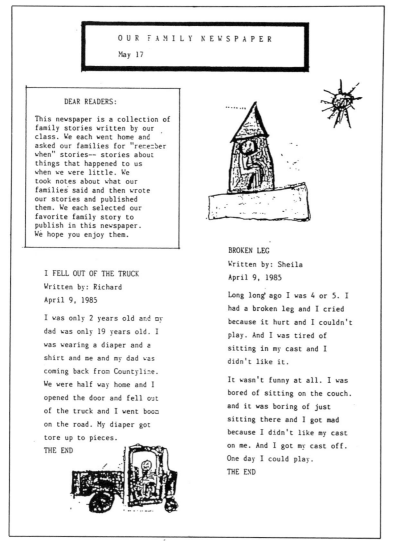

Figure 5. Family Story Newspaper

stories, they were also given opportunities to explore families in children's literature. The room was filled with books. Some were books of families telling stories, some were information books on families, and others were stories that involved families in some way. These books were explored by the children

Authoring through reading and discussing

In literature circles, we talk about the meaning of the books. We compare how they are the same and how they are different. We look at different versions of the same story. We discuss biographes, fairytales, books on Black history, and many more. Literature circles are a time to sit with other classmates and share our interpretations of the stories and what the ideas mean to us.

Alicia, Grade 3

Authoring through art and mathematics

Authoring through drama

as independent reading and some were read aloud and discussed at class meetings. Kathy introduced the author Pat Hutchins to the class and shared how Pat often wrote about her own family in her books. She read aloud five different books by Hutchins to the class and the children signed up for one of the books which they wanted to discuss with others. The children met for several days in their literature circles where they did some shared reading of the book they had chosen and then talked about issues related to their interpretations of the book. As they finished their discussions, some of the groups decided to spend time putting together a presentation about their book discussion for the rest of the class. The presentations included a mural showing different kinds of families, a skit about being the smallest in a family, a shared piece of writing about siblings fighting, a new version of *Rosie's Walk* (Hutchins, 1968), and a demonstration of sending a message down a whisper chain to see how it changes. These presentations were celebrated and received in the same way that published books were in that classroom.

At the end of each day, the class had a time where class members could share some of what they were learning about families. A variety of topics and questions came up during this sharing which led to other research and projects. Children conducted surveys of various aspects of their families such as the number of people in the family, family activities, pets, and the duties of different family members. Some children painted pictures about their families, others created collages or mobiles, and others created family shields. Each project had a particular purpose for the children in thinking about and portraying some aspect of their family life. Some of these projects were informal and were not displayed or even completed. Other projects involved children in careful consideration of how they were portraying their family and these projects underwent revision and were published by displaying them in some way in the classroom.

As different issues and situations came up in class discussions, reading, and writing, they often led to small skits or some type of role playing. These stayed informal and spur of the moment. They were not published by working to revise them and formally present them to others. The purpose of the skits was to give the class another way to think about their families and family relationships.

At the end of the focused study, the class had a celebration time where all of the books, projects, and publications were displayed and family members were invited to come to the classroom. The class also spent time reflecting on what they had learned about their families during this study and talking about the similarities and differences among families. Another topic of group reflection was on the research process of interviewing, taking notes, and representing their research through writing, graphs, and artwork.

Celebrating authorship and reflecting on learning

During this focusing study, the Authoring Cycle served as a curricular framework both for the study itself and for experiences within the study. When the children were involved in authoring family stories, the Authoring Cycle supported them as writers as they engaged in uninterrupted writing, shared rough drafts with others, and published some of their work. The Authoring Cycle also supported their experiences in reading as they read from a wide variety of books, explored some more intensively with others in Literature Circles, and shared their understandings with others in presentations. Their authoring through mathematics, art, and drama also was supported by the Authoring Cycle. Sometimes the publication was informal as in the skits where the acting out of the skit during class discussions was the publication. At other points, their presentations underwent revision and careful consideration before being presented in some type of formal form as occurred with the newspaper and some of the projects using art to portray aspects of the family. Throughout the family study, the cycle supported the children and their teachers in actively constructing their own meaning and using these constructions to propel their future learning.

Overlapping cycles of authoring in many sign systems

The Authoring Cycle not only supported different authoring engagements within the study, but was the broader

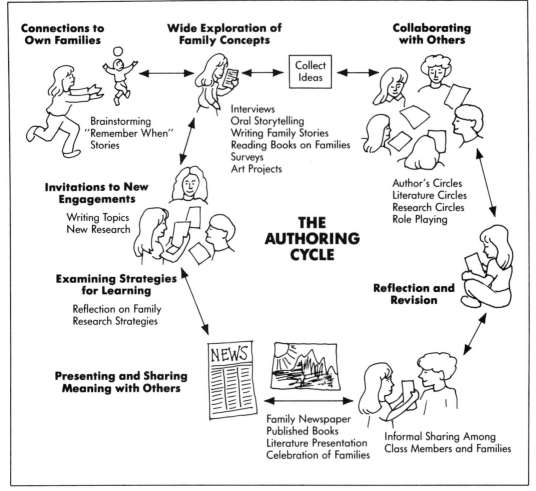

Figure 6. Authoring Cycle as Framework for Focused Study on Family

The authoring cycle as a framework for a broad focused study

curricular framework within which the study itself was developed (Figure 6). The study was based in children's own family experiences and began with many uninterrupted experiences exploring families as children read, wrote, drew, talked, acted, listened, and thought about this topic. Some of what they explored in these experiences became part of small or whole group interactions and was explored in more depth. The focused study came to a close with presentations, celebrations, and reflections which helped children pull together what they had learned, felt, and thought. Throughout the study, they participated in strategy lessons related to research strategies such as different ways to take notes and to use those notes in reporting research. While the class focus on family came to a close, the experiences from this study had opened up new invitations for children as they used these stories for new writing topics and used the research strategies in other class and individual studies.

In this classroom experience, the overarching Authoring Cycle supported the class members in authoring their own understandings about content, process, and purpose and had embedded within it many other cycles of authoring. Authoring, for the children and the teachers, was a metaphor for learning. They became authors of their own lives and learnings. Reading and writing were not just integrated into their subject area units but were tools they used along with other communication systems to learn. Throughout these experiences the teachers and students were actively involved as inquirers, exploring questions that made sense in their lives.

Authoring as a metaphor for learning

Learning-Centered Curriculum

If a curriculum is truly learning-centered, then that curriculum is based on inquiry and the search for questions that matter to us, whether we are adults or children. The function of curriculum is to support us in the inquiry process of searching for questions and ways of looking at those questions. Without inquiry, a sense of purpose and meaning in learning is lost and our natural inquisitiveness as learners is deadened. Instead of studying topics to gain bits and pieces of information, we ask our own questions and engage in inquiry. We learn to search for problems as well as explanations for our problems. We are both problem-posers and problem-solvers.

Curriculum as Inquiry

There are several beliefs that are fundamental to our position that curriculum is inquiry. The first is that learning is inquiry and inquiry is learning. In the past, the roles of researcher, teacher, and learner were always seen in a hierarchical relationship to each other. If we take a collaborative perspective on curriculum, then we have multiple roles available to each of us. Research is not an activity reserved only for university scholars. We define research as systematic inquiry which develops from being interested in the world, asking questions about aspects of the world that are puzzling, and investigating those questions and possible solutions. Both teachers and children should be involved in learning and re-

Learning and inquiry are the same process of posing and solving our own questions.

55

We need to search out the questions that matter to us.

The way I have grown as a thinker is that I think harder. I think through more about problems.

Chris, Grade 3

I think about problems that our world faces and I notice how authors solve the problems in their storybook worlds. I am a serious reader struggling for answers to solve my personal problem— my sister.

Mardell, Grade 3

searching, in searching out the questions that are significant in their lives.

A second belief is that inquiry questions must be framed by all who are intimately involved in that inquiry. Traditionally, research questions come from university researchers and are framed prior to the actual engagement. When the questions are framed ahead of time, the situation can be controlled in order to account for the variables. This viewpoint makes it hard for people to see themselves as researchers and inquirers because their role becomes a passive one and their insights are not valued. Whether the people involved are classroom teachers participating in a university research study or children participating in a theme unit in a particular content area, they are excluded from the process of searching out their own questions. They are passive participants. As teachers, we have been expected to be consumers of research on questions that we see as peripheral to our lives as educators and from which our perspective has been excluded. Children experience the same disconnectedness as they are involved in content area studies where the teacher has already determined what will be explored and how that exploration will take place.

Other people's questions do not interest us as much as our own questions. We are not born passive. As argued earlier, curiosity is natural to our lives. We are born researchers. Teachers are encouraged to be passive by curriculum guides, teacher's manuals, standardized tests, classroom furniture, school schedules, and tradition. In turn, this passivity is passed on to our students. Much of school consists of learning sets of skills and information instead of pursuing questions that matter to the learner and that involve the use of various strategies and knowledge.

We underestimate children when we think they do not have questions that are of significance to them. Several years ago Kathy asked a group of first graders to share what they had always wanted to know. The range and depth of their questions surprised her. They asked questions such as:

How does a telephone work?
How do clouds move around?
How do you ride a horse and not fall off?
Who went to the moon first?
Why does the ocean have waves?
How does an artist become an artist?
How do people grow?
How old is the world?
How did dinosaurs get made?
How fast do horses run?
Who made the first baby doll?
What do dinosaurs do?
How do you make hard books?
How did the world get made?
How were mountains made?
How do you make books?

(Short, 1986)

Search out the questions that matter to you as a teacher and a learner. You might start out by asking yourself in what ways you are encouraged to be active or passive in your current teaching situation. Think of your students and whether they are encouraged to be active or passive thinkers and inquirers in your classroom. During this past school year, what were the questions about learning, teaching, or curriculum that kept coming to your mind? What were situations or responses that puzzled or surprised you? Take a moment and jot down some of your questions. What do you want to know or understand better in your classroom?

I bring problems from home to school. The ideas float around my mind. I talk about them and I solve my problems.

Megan, Grade 3

....

My current questions:

How might I go about investigating my questions?

....

We need the opportunity to think with people we trust.

A third belief is that trust forms the basis for the continuing engagement in inquiry. Traditionally, the researcher has been in a tutorial role, passing down information and decisions to the other participants. We should be distrustful of any decision making in which we were not involved. All of us think. All of us have real questions about which we are thinking. All of us can make invitations to others around us about new ways of thinking.

We know each other so good that we feel free to come up to each other and ask questions. We trust each other.

Kim, Grade 3

Just as children need collaborative groups of other learners whom they trust to help them think through rough draft ideas in their writing and reading, these groups support all of us as learners in thinking through questions. As teachers, we need collaborative groups of other educators and our students to think about questions related to classroom life and learning. Children need collaborative groups where they can explore their questions about how the world works. Within these collaborative groups, diversity is valued and each individual is seen as bringing a unique persective.

We are all special in some way. It takes courage and time to learn and get along.

Mardell, Grade 3

As teachers, we need others to think and inquire with us rather than more inservice courses where we listen and someone else tells us what to do with our classrooms (Watson, Burke, & Harste, 1989). Many teachers are exploring options such as writing groups where teachers gather before or after school for coffee and to share their writing with each other. Other teachers have formed literature groups where they read and discuss children's books or adult literature. Still others have formed study groups which meet after school on a regular basis so teachers can share what is happening in their classrooms and discuss where they might go next. Teachers in these groups often choose a common issue on which to focus and read articles or books together which help them think through these issues. Sometimes these groups are school-based while other groups are composed of teachers from different schools who have a common theoretical base or set of concerns.

I think it's neat because my teacher shares with other teachers and they learn from each other.

Brooks, Grade 2

Who are other educators and learners who you trust and who might join you in a collaborative group to inquire about questions important to your lives in school?

. . . .

My Potential Collaborators:

. . . .

A fourth belief is that the purpose of engaging in inquiry is exploration. Traditionally, the purpose for inquiry has been seen as confirming what is already known and making that information conventional. If, as we argued earlier, inquiry is seen as question asking and seeking, then we do not need to worry about the responses. Progress is measured by having new questions that we are ready to ask rather than answers we can pass on to others. The answers will take care of themselves. Our concern is the questions. The answers we create from inquiry will last only as long as we need time to ask new questions and until more compelling theories and beliefs come into existence. The sign that a university or teacher research study or a child's expert study has been successful is whether it ends with the generation of new questions as well as new understandings for everyone involved.

The goal of inquiry is to generate new questions, not eliminate them.

The questions and alternative perspectives keep us going. We do not inquire to eliminate alternatives. We are trying to find more functional answers, and to create diversity and broaden our thinking. Research is not intended to eliminate questions but to generate new questions. In any learning situation, the process which supports this systematic questioning and inquiry is evaluation.

I used to think work was hard. But this year, it is easy. When you are in the middle of something, we don't quit. We collect more information about it.

Brian, Grade 3

Evaluation as Reflective Inquiry

There is a final dimension about curriculum and inquiry which needs to be raised. Some readers might have noticed that there is one word that we have not found necessary to use as we talked about both our envisioned and enacted curricula. That word is evaluation.

That omission is due neither to an oversight or to the fact that we do not see evaluation as serving a significant function in curriculum. It has to do with the function we see evaluation as playing.

Before we share some of our thoughts about the function of evaluation in curriculum, spend a few minutes jotting down the first thoughts that come into your mind when you hear the word "evaluation." After you have written down your connections to the term "evaluation," make a list of the evaluation experiences which you currently use in your classroom.

. . . .

My thoughts about evaluation:

Ways in which I currently evaluate:

. . . .

Traditionally, evaluation has been seen as an outside force that is imposed upon the curriculum generally and the learner specifically. It has been externally imposed because of several assumptions—that the questions which drive the curriculum must be supplied by outside recognized experts, that the vast majority of what is to be learned is already known, digested, and organized, and that there are acknowledged correct responses to the curricular questions which are to be asked. You will recognize that these are assumptions which we rejected in constructing our beliefs about learning and our visions of curriculum.

These assumptions have led many educators to associate evaluation with grades, testing, and accountability, not reflection on our inquiry and learning. In their view, evaluation occurs after learning takes place and is used by administrators and the community to hold teachers and students accountable for what is taught and learned in a school context. As our beliefs about learning and curriculum change and new models for curriculum are developed, our beliefs about evaluation also need to change. Evaluation is part of the curriculum, not separate from it, and therefore needs to be guided by the same beliefs that guide our thinking as we work with students to develop curriculum. Many of the evaluation tools currently used in schools are based in a different set of beliefs and are no longer relevant to supporting inquiry within a learning community.

Whether learning is formal or informal, no one who engages in learning as a personally significant inquiry does so without monitoring what and how they are learning. It is this self monitoring which we believe fuels the powerful function of strategy instruction in the Authoring Cycle curriculum. In these circumstances, evaluation is no longer seen as something imposed on the learner, but becomes a reflective perspective taken by learners. Within our curriculum, all evaluation is seen as starting with self-evaluation. So, in effect, we have been establishing the criteria for taking an evaluative stance every time that we have taken consideration of the role which reflection plays in learning.

Evaluation as a reflective stance taken by learners

At the heart of e**valu**ation is the word "value." When we evaluate, we make a value judgment—we decide what we value for ourselves and others and make decisions based on those values. Evaluation is what allows us to move our inquiry ahead, not what someone else imposes from the outside. Evaluation involves gathering the information needed to continue moving in our learning and inquiry. The goal of evaluation is thus to give inquirers the insights they need to guide their next inquiry. Evaluation is not separate from learning but involves taking a reflective perspective on our own and others' learning.

Evaluation highlights what we value as learners.

When I'm finished, I think about what I need to know next.

Marita, Grade 3

The major issue in evaluation is not subjectivity versus objectivity. All evaluation is subjective, regardless of whether it involves collections of numbers. Standardized tests are subjective in the decisions that are made by test makers about what to include on the test out of the wide range of ideas and knowledge available and in what are chosen as the correct answers. On the other hand, just watching children without recording those observations in some way does not give teachers or students a way to stand back and reflect on the inquiry which is occurring. In order for evaluation to support inquiry, learners need a systematic way to gather, record, and analyze what is occurring during learning. They do not need a set of percentages.

As we searched for a new model for evaluation as the basis for inquiry and curriculum, we returned to our beliefs about learning. Carolyn developed a model of evaluation which has been useful to both of us in our continued work with curriculum (Figure 7). As we argued in the earlier section on our beliefs, learning involves being engaged in active doing and in changing our perspective through reflection and interaction with others. Evaluation then consists of examining the process of learning from a variety of perspectives.

Evaluation involves the dimensions of process and perspective.

Learning can be examined on the basis of two dimensions: process and perspective. Each of these dimensions is composed of three aspects. The three aspects of the learning process which need to be considered in evaluation are intent, engagement, and artifact. *Intent* refers to why learners do something: their purposes for becoming involved in an engagement. Learners do not do something for no reason. Even though they may not be able to explicitly state their purpose, they always act with intention (Harste, Woodward, & Burke, 1984). *Engagement* refers to the actual doing: the fulfilling of the intent through an experience. *Artifact* refers to the product which is present at the end of the process. Product is thus part of process, not set in opposition to process, and functions to serve as a history of the process.

The process of learning can be examined from three different perspectives. Each of these perspectives involves looking at learning from someone's viewpoint. All valuing of learning begins with the perspective of *Self* as learners evaluate their own learning in order to move forward. *Collabo-*

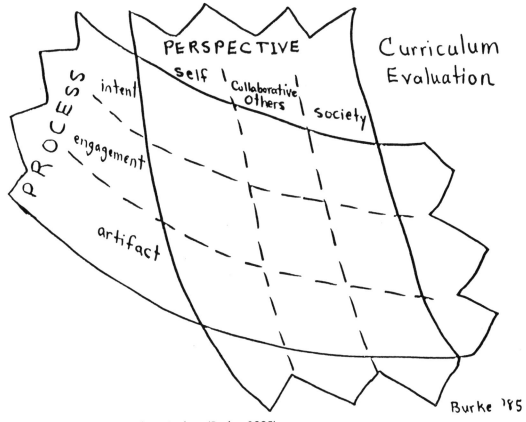

Figure 7. Evaluation and curriculum (Burke, 1985).

rative Others are individuals involved in the learning setting who know the learner well and who view the learner from a close personal perspective. In the classroom setting, collaborative others are those who are taking some of the same risks and are involved in the same inquiry as the learner. *Society* is a more distant perspective and is the one most closely associated with accountability. This perspective is taken by people who are interested and have an investment in schools but who are not collaboratively involved with individual learners.

In order for evaluation to provide a well-rounded profile of learning, all aspects of the process of learning—intent, engagement, and artifact—must be considered from all three perspectives—self, collaborative others, and society. The aspects create a grid or picture which can be used to capture the potentials for evaluation that are embedded in our curriculum. This picture has allowed us to recognize the evaluative potential in engagements that already exist within the curriculum and that will prompt our development of other potential evaluative opportunities.

In most schools, report cards, standardized tests, and textbook tests are the major forms of evaluation. These measures come from the perspective of society and examine artifacts. Most of what is currently done in evaluation is thus focused in one small corner of the grid. There are many other sources of evaluation that need to be considered, especially if educators want evaluation to inform and advance our inquiry and learning.

The society perspective is a distant stance taken by people who have an investment and interest in schools.

While society needs to have schools report on the artifacts of learning, the types of report cards and tests that are currently used violate much of what is known about learning. Society does need to have the products of learning available, but schools need to devise other ways of making these artifacts available. Some schools, for example, are using district-wide *Portfolios* as a way to share artifacts that more fully reflect the processes and intents of learners.

Society rarely considers the engagement of learners in the actual process of learning or learners' intents for learning. Experiences such as *Young Authors' Conferences* or *Parents' Day* can give society a sense of process if parents and/or administrators are involved with students in actual writing and doing as part of these experiences. Intent for learning can be communicated to society through *Parents' Nights* and *Parent Conferences* where teachers explain the curriculum and their intentions for the learning in that classroom. Intent can also be communicated when student statements about their goals for learning are included as part of the reporting process to parents. Usually, however, society communicates its intents for learning through curriculum guides and textbooks without hearing the intents of teachers or students.

A collaborative other perspective is taken as learners create a community where each feels a personal connection to others in that community through engagement in shared inquiry. Intent from a collaborative other perspective involves teachers or peers trying to understand other learners' intentions for their learning. Intent is often conveyed through *Reader and Writer Interviews* focused on understanding the learner's beliefs and practices about reading and writing. *Attitude and Interest Surveys* can also give a sense of intent.

> Collaborative others have a close personal perspective and are involved in inquiry with learners.

Many of the alternative forms of evaluation that have been developed in the past few years look at learners as they are engaged in learning from the perspective of collaborative others. Different forms of oral *Miscue Analysis*, *Running Records*, *Print Awareness Tasks*, *Anecdotal Records*, *Field Notes*, *Observation Checklists*, *Videotapes*, and *Audiotapes* are all examples of tools used to look at learners as they are actually engaged in learning. *Literature Circles* and *Authors' Circles* often involve peers evaluating each other's "in process" constructions of meaning in reading or writing through group dialogue.

Examples of collaborative others evaluating artifacts include teachers and peers reviewing children's *Authors' Folders* and *Learning Logs* to look at changes over time, use of *Holistic Scoring* to evaluate writing, and analysis of *Retellings* following reading. The *Charts*, *Webs*, *Graphs*, *Notes*, and *Presentations* often produced as part of a study are artifacts which can be examined. *Outside Editors* involve students in evaluating the artifacts of their peers.

The perspective of self allows learners to understand themselves better and become independent thinkers who are not totally dependent on the judgments of others. Grades on report cards and the comments of others are no longer their only source of information about themselves. They have many other ways of seeing and evaluating themselves as learners to

> All valuing of learning begins with the perspective of self.

know what they are learning and where they are moving. The evaluation devices used for self-evaluation also give collaborative others further information but from an insider perspective rather than just the perspective of an observer.

Learners get a sense of their own intentions for learning when they *Brainstorm* before beginning a focused study on what they know about a particular topic and what they want to know. *Research Journals* allow them to keep track of their changing questions and intentions for learning as they pursue their study. Learners need devices to get them in touch with themselves and what they are currently thinking and want to pursue. *Authors' Circles* can play this function for authors who discover their own intentions for a piece of writing when faced with suggestions from others which violate those intentions.

Learning Logs, *Literature Logs*, and various types of written *Self-Evaluations* allow learners to reflect on their process of learning. While these same devices are viewed as artifacts by collaborative others, they capture a process of learning for the learner. One self-evaluation strategy involves using pictures taken during learning activities and having students write about what they were thinking and doing when the picture was taken.

Authors Folders, *Lists* of books read or written, and *Portfolios* of selected work are all ways learners can collect artifacts of their growth over time. These artifacts, in turn, can be viewed from the perspective of collaborative others. On the model in Figure 8, many of the evaluation devices that are placed into a particular box could occur in other parts of the grid depending on who is viewing or using that device at a particular point in time.

After examining this evaluation model, go back to your list of ways you currently evaluate in your teaching setting. Put your list into the empty grid (Figure 7). Does your system of evaluation provide a well-rounded picture of learning or are there empty sections on the grid? The grid can be used to examine the evaluation strategies for all learners: students,

I revise by changing some things that don't go there in the story so it sounds good. Sometimes I take ideas and sometimes I don't.

Josh, Grade 3

My portfolio is kind of like a safe. I think of important stuff I want to keep. I look at it and can tell it's good. At the end of the year, I keep it and remember it.

Jason, Grade 3

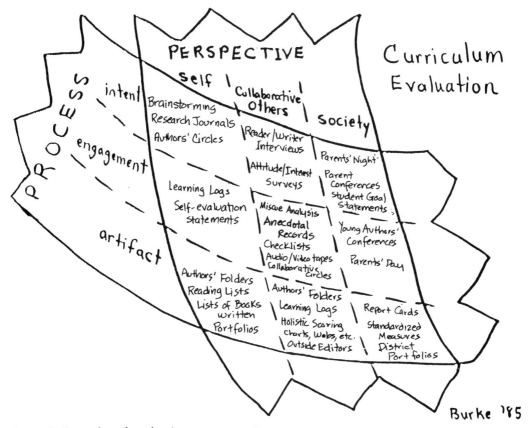

Figure 8. Examples of evaluation engagements.

teachers, administrators, parents, school board members, etc. Does the teacher evaluation system used in your school, for example, focus on the intents, engagements, and artifacts of a teacher's learning from the perspectives of self, collaborative others, and society or is only a society perspective involved?

This model of evaluation highlights the need for many different perspectives from which to view evaluation. All of the evaluation opportunities which are part of this grid can *not* be later funneled into a standardized form to report to society because these forms offer only one perspective. Taking multiple perspectives allows learners to value and make commitments to learning. When value is placed on certain kinds of experiences and we have the opportunity to monitor our learning, we are empowered to act. We know the direction we are going and have the strategies we need to get there. We are authors of our own lives.

Becoming authors of our own lives

Traditionally, schools have assumed that first teachers teach, then learners engage in doing, and finally teachers test them to see if they have really learned what was taught. Our beliefs about learning have led us to a different view of these relationships. Our primary focus is on engaging learners in meaningful learning and evaluating that learning as it occurs in order to inform the teaching occurring in a learning community. We do not assume that teachers are the only ones engaged in teaching or evaluating. The social relationships between teachers and students have been drastically changed within the community. The classroom is not teacher-centered or student-centered but *learning-centered* with teachers and students working collaboratively in supporting each other's learning and inquiry.

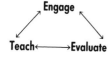

Mardell, a third grader, wrote a self-evaluation of her learning several months into the school year (Figure 9). She speaks powerfully about how the curriculum in her classroom had allowed her and her classmates to collaborate with their teacher in designing a generative learning environment.

I used to think that in school you had to learn everything the teacher said to learn. This year, we keep asking new questions instead of stopping our learning.

Anna, Grade 4

For any curricular framework to be useful and generative, it must support all learners in that community (adults and children) in inquiry. Both teachers and students need time to explore, to collaborate with others, to present their understandings to others, to reflect on and monitor their inquiry, and to create new questions. All learners need structures that support them in this inquiry process. When teachers see themselves as active inquirers, then they can collaborate with their students in creating classrooms that are active places of inquiry.

A curriculum framework must support all learners in inquiry.

The Authoring Cycle is a curriculum framework that we

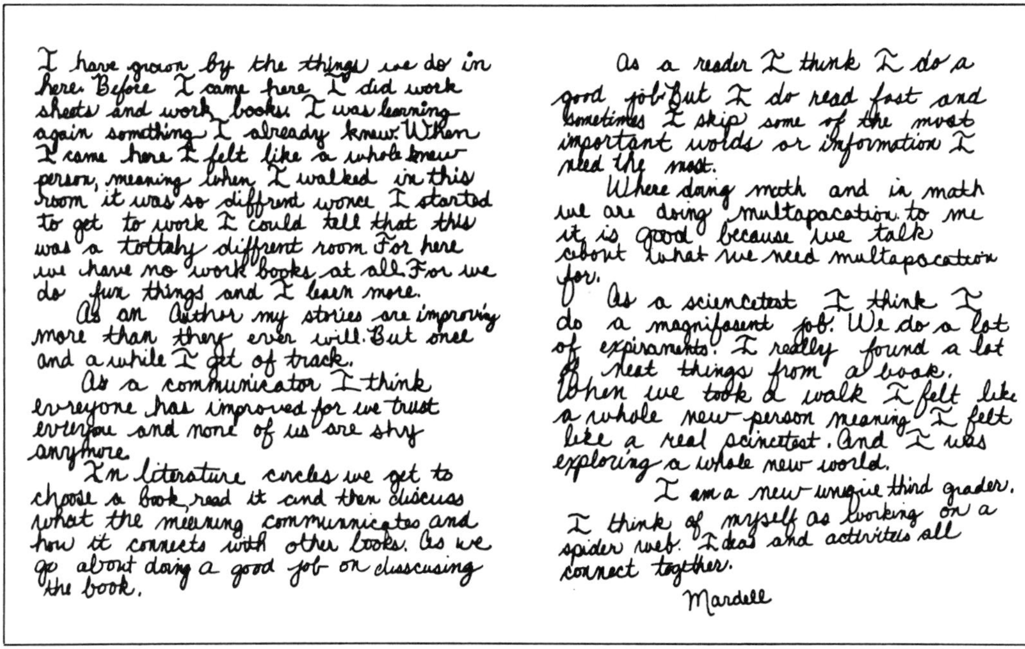

I have grown by the things we do in here. Before I came here I did work sheets and work books. I was learning again something I already knew. When I came here I felt like a whole new person, meaning when I walked in this room it was so diffrent wonce I started to get to work I could tell that this was a tottaly diffrent room. For here we have no work books at all. For we do fun things and I learn more.

As an author my stories are improving more than they ever will. But once and a while I get of track.

As a communicator I think evreyone has improved for we trust everyone and none of us are shy anymore.

In literature circles we get to choose a book, read it and then discuss what the meaning communnicates and how it connects with other books. As we go about doing a good job on discussing the book.

As a reader I think I do a good job but I do read fast and sometimes I skip some of the most important wolds or information I need the most.

Where dong moth and in math we are doing multapocation to me it is good because we talk about what we need multapocation for.

As a sciencetest I think I do a magnifesent job. We do a lot of expiraments. I really found a lot of neat things from a book. When we took a walk I felt like a whole new person meaning I felt like a real scinetest. And I was exploring a whole new world.

I am a new unique third grader. I think of myself as working on a spider web. Ideas and activities all connect together.

Mardell

Figure 9. Mardell's Self-evaluation.

have found helpful in supporting our inquiry. We have presented our beliefs and the curricular framework we developed from those beliefs not as a model for others to adopt but as a process of thinking about curriculum which others can use as they think about curriculum and inquiry in their own classroom settings.

Curriculum is a purposeful intent to empower ourselves and others. The answers to the three questions posed at the beginning of this book on the nature of learners, the conditions that support learning, and the evaluation of learning provide a theoretical framework for the realization of a working model of learning.

The important issue is not the specific organizational device that forms the curriculum in a particular setting but whether that curriculum has been purposefully devised to provide the potential for empowerment of all learners. The

I used to feel like a straight ruler. Now I can be a slinky. I can be creative and different.

Jeff, Grade 6

curriculum should be the place where the learning in which we are engaged in the present acts to vitalize our past and empower our future. This is best done by building on the natural motivations of learners and by offering invitations which create a supportive context for empowerment.

WHAT WE LEARNED THIS YEAR
1. *Share your ideas with others.*
2. *Tell others your opinions.*
3. *Think about what you do and why you do it.*
4. *You don't always have to be right.*
5. *We can learn from our mistakes.*
6. *It matters how you learn.*
7. *Learn from other kids and not just teachers.*
8. *Know where and how you learn.*
9. *Learn in new and different ways.*
10. *It is easy to change if you try.*
11. *Share your learning with others.*
12. *Don't be afraid to learn.*
13. *Don't keep your ideas locked up inside of you.*
14. *Spread your ideas around.*
15. *Keeping adding to your mind.*
16. *Never stop learning.*

Brainstormed List, Grade 3 class

Now I want to work because I know I never will stop learning. I have a scrapbook mind that I keep adding on to.

Megan, Grade 3

REFERENCES

Boslough, J. 1985. *Stephen Hawking's Universe*. New York: Morrow.

Burke, C. 1985. "Parenting, Teaching, and Learning as a Collaborative Venture." *Language Arts*, 62 (8), 836–844.

Dewey, J. 1938. *Experience and Education*. New York: Collier Books.

Fleck, L. 1935. *Genesis and Development of a Scientific Fact*. Chicago: University of Chicago Press.

Goodman, Y. 1978. "Kidwatching: An Alternative to Testing," *The Education Digest*.

Goodman, Y. and Burke, C. 1980. *Reading Strategies: Focus on Comprehension*. New York: Richard C. Owen.

Harste, J. and K. Short, with C. Burke. 1988. *Creating Classrooms for Authors: The Reading-Writing Connection*. Portsmouth, N.H.: Heinemann.

Harste, J., V. Woodward, and C. Burke. 1984. *Language Stories and Literacy Lessons*. Portsmouth, N. H.: Heinemann.

Hutchins, P. 1968. *Rosie's Walk*. New York: Macmillan.

Rosen, H. 1984. *Stories and Meaning*. London: National Association for the Teaching of English.

Rylant, C. 1985. *The Relatives Came*. New York: Bradbury.

Short, K. 1986. *Literacy as a Collaborative Experience*. Bloomington, Ind.: Unpublished doctoral dissertation, Indiana University.

Smith, F. 1981. "Demonstrations, Engagement, and Sensitivity: A Revised Approach to Language Learning." *Language Arts, 58*, 103–112.

Smith F. 1987. *Insult to Intelligence*. New York: Arbor House.

Spiegel, D. 1981. *Reading for Pleasure: Guidelines*. Newark, Del.: International Reading Association.

Vygotsky L. 1978. *Mind in Society*. Cambridge, Mass.: Harvard University Press.

Watson, D., C. Burke, and J. Harste., 1989. *Whole Language: Inquiring Voices*. New York: Scholastic.